ning

DATE			

WITHDRAWN

GAYLORD S

Peer Assisted Learning

A Practical Guide for Teachers

Keith Topping

BROOKLINE BOOKS • NEWTON, MA 02464

Copyright © 2001 by Brookline Books

Library of Congress Cataloging-in-Publication Data

Topping, Keith J.
  Peer assisted learning: a practical guide for teachers / Keith Topping.
      p. cm.
Includes bibliographical references.
  ISBN 1-57129-085-0 (pbk.)
  1. Peer-group tutoring of students–Handbooks, manuals, etc. I. Title.
    LB1031.5.T66 2000
    371.39'4–dc21

                              00-012343

Printed in the USA by The P.A. Hutchison Company, Mayfield, PA
10 9 8 7 6 5 4 3 2

Published by
BROOKLINE BOOKS
P.O. Box 97 • Newton, MA 02464
Order toll-free: 1-800-666-BOOK

Contents

1

Introduction

"Peer Assisted Learning"—what do we mean by that? Responding to this question, some teachers will:

- Think only of peer tutoring
- Or even think only of a particular kind of peer tutoring in a particular curriculum area,
- Assume tutoring involves some kind of pull-out or withdrawal from the mainstream,
- Regard tutoring as something only selected, older, higher-achieving students can do,
- Be concerned about tutors not using their time to best effect, and
- Consider tutoring a much inferior alternative to professional teaching.

In fact, Peer Assisted Learning:

- Includes many different forms of peer tutoring,
- Includes other arrangements for students to help other students to learn, in addition to peer tutoring,
- Is often used in core curriculum areas like literacy, math, science and information technology, but can be used in any curricular area with a little imagination and organization,

- Can and should be socially inclusive, involving a broad spectrum of students (often in-class and on a whole-class basis), avoiding tutor elitism and tutee stigmatization,
- Can and should be organized so that *both helpers and helped* make substantial gains in learning achievement, in addition to any motivational or social gains,
- Can and should involve students of all levels of ability *as both helpers and helped*—since everyone has some island of competence and everyone learns through the process of helping another to learn.
- Is a form of active and interactive and individualized learning that is planned, managed and supervised by professional teachers— complementing professional teaching and adding value to it,
- Has been shown by research to be one of the most effective ways of raising student achievement, when properly organized and implemented,
- Typically requires little by way of new materials, and has been shown by research to be one of the most cost-effective ways of raising student achievement.

This book is a practical guide for teachers in how to plan and effectively implement different kinds of Peer Assisted Learning in any area of the curriculum – in a way which integrates with and complements direct teaching by professionals. It covers many different kinds of peer tutoring, and also other kinds of Peer Assisted Learning (PAL) such as peer modeling, peer monitoring of learning behavior and peer assessment of learning products. It considers the use of PAL with students of all ages, abilities, and linguistic and cultural backgrounds, organized so that both helper and helped gain in achievement. It is solidly based on decades of research evidence and practical experience. It builds upon Keith Topping's previous (1988) book for Brookline ("The Peer Tutoring Handbook"), but substantially updates and goes far beyond it.

Peer Assisted Learning can be defined as the acquisition of knowledge and skill through active helping and supporting among status equals or matched companions. PAL involves people from similar social groupings who are not professional teachers helping each other to learn and learning themselves by so doing.

Peer Assisted Learning (PAL) includes:

- Peer Tutoring: characterized by specific role taking as tutor or tutee, with high focus on curriculum content and usually specific procedures for interaction, in which participants are trained.
- Peer Modelling: the provision of a competent exemplar of desirable learning behavior by a member or members of a group with the intention that others in the group will imitate it.
- Peer Monitoring: peers observing and checking the process learning behaviors of others in the group with respect to appropriateness and effectiveness.
- Peer Assessment: peers formatively and qualitatively evaluating the products or outcomes of learning of others in the group.
- PAL also includes Peer Education and Peer Counselling, but these more complex methods are not dealt with in this book (see Topping & Ehly, 1998).

This book does not deal with the more general methods of "cooperative learning" and "mentoring". In "cooperative learning", typically the participants are working in parallel toward some common goal, rather than primarily, specifically and consciously helping each other's learning. In "mentoring", typically the focus is not directly upon curricular achievement, and the helpers themselves are not expected to gain.

In this book, the long history of Peer Assisted Learning and the mass of research evidence on its effectiveness are reviewed, but only briefly, since this is readily available in greater depth elsewhere if required. The advantages and disadvantages of Peer Assisted Learning (PAL) are summarized, and the processes through which it has its effects outlined. A typology of different kinds of Peer Assisted Learning then gives teachers a clear framework (or "menu") for choosing the PAL method most appropriate for their needs and context. The core of the book is the extensive guide to planning and implementing the chosen PAL method effectively. This is coupled with a detailed reproducible Planning Format, useful for structuring preliminary thinking and subsequent planning meetings, and for recording organizational decisions. Reproducible information for parents is also included. Ways of evaluating PAL projects within limited time and resources are then reviewed, given the frequent need to demonstrate cost-effectiveness locally. Embedding and extending PAL so it is more than an ephemeral novelty is discussed. Further readings, sources and resources (both paper-based and from the Internet) are recommended.

It has been said that:

WE LEARN...

10% of what we READ
20% of what we HEAR
30% of what we SEE
50% of what we both SEE and HEAR
70% of what we DISCUSS with others
80% of what we EXPERIENCE personally
90% of what we TEACH others

When you have read this book, find an opportunity to see a PAL program in action, discuss the ideas in the book with your colleagues, try out PAL in your own classroom, and discuss what happens with your colleagues and with your students – and then teach your colleagues some of what you have learned. Then you will really have learned it.

2

The History Of Peer Assisted Learning (PAL)

"Make your friends your teachers, and mingle the pleasures of conversation with the advantages of instruction"

– Baltasar Gracian (1647)

Arrangements which have some of the features of present day peer assisted learning have been reported from ancient Rome and in the early practices of Judaism. 'Monitors' were employed in Elizabethan grammar schools during the latter half of the sixteenth century. The grouping of pupils by chronological age only became common practice towards the middle of the eighteenth century. Prior to that childhood was not perceived as a separate category of life, and once past the age of 5-7 years, the child became part of the world of adults, acquiring work and social skills by participation in informal apprenticeship (Allen, 1976).

The Bell-Lancaster System

The first *systematic* use of peer tutoring in the world is undoubtedly associated with the name of Andrew Bell. In 1789, Bell was appointed superintendent of a charity school for the orphaned sons of soldiers at Madras. Bell found the school's teachers resistant to some of the new educational ideas he wished to introduce, and so he turned to experimenting with peer tutors using these new ideas. He rapidly became aware that the systematic use of children to teach other children was an innovation of greater significance than the new ideas themselves.

In Bell's system, each class was paired into tutors and tutees, and to each class was attached an 'assistant teacher' to supervise and instruct the tutors. The assistant teacher reported to a teacher, who reported to an 'usher', who in turn reported to the 'school master'. Every member of the school community had a specified role and clearly defined tasks. Bell's school incorporated classes in which pupils were grouped according to achievement rather than chronological age, and pupils were promoted or demoted in a way akin to the workings of the 'grade' system in North America.

Bell found the motivation and behavior of both tutors and tutees much improved, remarking: "the very moment you nominate a boy a tutor, you have exalted him in his own eyes, and given him a character to support". The effects of this system in raising pupil attainment appeared to be substantial. Thus Bell (1797) reported: "Firsken, of 12 years and 8 months, with his assistants of 7, 8, 9 and 11 years of age, has taught boys of 4, 5 and 6 years to read *The Spectator* distinctly, and spell every word accurately as they go along." However, Bell equally emphasized the social and emotional benefits of his scheme, claiming that it 'cultivates the best dispositions of the heart by teaching children to take an early and well-directed interest in the welfare of one another'.

In 1801 Joseph Lancaster opened the Borough Road School for 350 disadvantaged boys in London. He arranged classes on the basis of attainment in individual curriculum areas, and deployed "monitors" and assistant monitors to each class to ensure that the pupils helped each other. He used highly structured curriculum materials, reducing the need for a substantial differential in achievement between tutor and tutee in the curriculum task to be mastered. Lancaster (1803) was a vigorous publicist for the new methods, and Bell reported in 1817 that in England and Wales about 100,000 children were being taught by the 'Bell-Lancaster' system.

The ideas of Bell and Lancaster were taken up in the New World, some Eastern European countries (including Russia), and in Western territorial possessions around the world. However, the popularity of the system gradually waned over the years, not least because the state began to provide money for public education and teaching became increasingly professionalized. As with many innovations, it might be that some subsequent imitators lacked the rigor of the original proponents. It seems that the tutors themselves were given little specific training, acquiring their skills on an apprenticeship basis, and this may have proved inadequate in the long run.

Large Classes and Small Schools

As education became more accessible for all in the western world, large classes nonetheless created the desirability, if not the necessity, of deploying at least some of the children as tutors. Equally, the one-teacher village school was once very common, although today it is usually only found in sparsely populated rural areas. In such schools, 'vertical' or 'family' grouping is necessary; children of all ages receiving instruction within a single room. In such situations, the younger pupils of greater ability automatically have access to more advanced instruction, while less able pupils automatically have access to frequent review and preview of material. Furthermore, the mixed-age classroom presents an ideal opportunity for older and more able pupils to assist younger and less able pupils with learning.

In 1974 Allen and Devin-Sheehan surveyed the use of children as tutors in 110 rural schools which still functioned with a single teacher. Some form of tutoring was reported to take place on a fairly regular basis in 30 percent of the schools, and in another 25 percent there were similar informal arrangements. Most of the formal tutoring was on a one-to-one basis, although tutors frequently worked with more than one tutee during the week. Same gender and opposite gender pairings were equally frequent, while the age differential in pairings ranged from zero to five years.

Whilst never widespread after the late 1800s peer tutoring projects could still be found through into the twentieth century. For example, Reigert (1916) described the implementation of the Bell-Lancaster system in the schools of New York City.

Resurgence in the USA

During the 1960s there was a resurgence of interest in peer tutoring, as attention in the United States and elsewhere focused on problems of under-achievement in the public schools.

The 'Tutorial Community' of Melaragno and Newmark incorporated the systematic and universal use of peers as mediators of instruction, with specification of professional teachers as managers of instruction rather than direct instructors, a programmed curriculum based on task-analyzed behavioral objectives, and a training facility for those wishing to implement similar programs elsewhere. The program was targeted on ethnic minority low-income populations. Melaragno and Newmark also took care to include a systematic evaluation in their program development, and their work still makes inspiring reading (e.g., in Allen, 1976).

Gartner, Kohler and Riessman (1971) documented this resurgence of interest in peer tutoring, setting it in the context of the anti-poverty and compensatory education politics of the era, with much interest in the affective and attitudinal outcomes which might accrue. These authors reported on, or referred to, hundreds of locally-based programs. By 1970, more than 200 school districts had adopted some type of tutoring program. By 1974, Melaragno claimed that over 10,000 elementary schools had some form of peer tutoring program.

Resurgence in the UK and World-wide

In 1975 Charconnet produced a UNESCO report reviewing various systems of peer tutoring with reference to their application in developing countries. Interest was also aroused in the United Kingdom, where in 1979 Sinclair Goodlad published *Learning by Teaching: An Introduction to Tutoring* and Carol Fitz-Gibbon did much to promote peer tutoring (e.g., Fitz-Gibbon and Reay, 1982). In the UK, the 1980s were characterized by a massive growth of interest in parental involvement in children's reading at home (Topping and Wolfendale, 1985; Wolfendale and Topping, 1996). Out of this came the development of various structured techniques for non-professional tutoring in reading, which were simple yet effective, were easily trained and could be applied without any need for specialized structured material. Two of these in particular ('Paired Reading' and 'Pause, Prompt and Praise') were also rapidly deployed for peer assisted learning.

The Future

The drive for ever higher standards of attainment continues apace, coupled with concerns about the development of social and emotional intelligence, and increased emphasis on evidence-based education. In this context, Peer Assisted Learning attracts more and more attention, since it meets all these needs without significant extra resources. PAL is also diversifying in all kinds of ways, including through exploration of peer modeling, peer monitoring and peer assessment.

The impact of information and communications technology necessitates a shift in the role of the teacher from linear transmitter of finite knowledge to manager of effective learning. Peer Assisted Learning fits extremely well into this new conception of pedagogy—it is indeed fit for the future.

3

Research Evidence
for Effectiveness

Teachers are often more likely to implement a new method if they have
seen it in action in a neighboring school, or if they have had good
reports of it from somebody they know in person. Busy practitioners
often regard the research literature with a degree of suspicion, as being
of doubtful relevance to life in the classroom. However, research evidence
can be useful, to:

- Reassure yourself that a method has a good chance of making a
  difference,
- Persuade colleagues and senior managers to cooperate,
- Encourage students to cooperate,
- Encourage parents of students to cooperate,
- Show what aspects of the method and organization are crucial to
  effectiveness,
- Make a case for funding,
- Keep the school inspectors happy,
- And so on...

Peer assisted learning is one of the best evidenced methods in
education, consistently showing not only high effectiveness in a number
of areas of student functioning, but also very high cost-effectiveness.

There is a great deal of good quality research on the subject of peer tutoring, in particular, far too much to consider in detail here. Those who need more detail should follow up the references given below.

Early Reviews Of Research on Peer Tutoring

As renewed interest in peer tutoring rapidly grew, many overviews were published (e.g., Gartner, et al., 1971; Rosenbaum, 1973; Klaus, 1975; Wilkes, 1975; Bloom, 1975; Eberwein, et al., 1976).

Feldman, Devin-Sheehan and Allen (1976) offered the first rigorous review of research (also see Devin Sheehan, et al., 1976). Some well-controlled research had been conducted. Students with a variety of handicaps and problems had benefited from serving as tutors, and a number of studies had found that low achievers in reading made significant gains in reading ability following their tutoring of younger children. It was clear that tutoring reliably resulted in improved attainment, but the evidence for social or personality benefits was more variable and often based on less reliable measures.

A predominant belief was that same-sex pairs facilitated tutoring, but there was little empirical support for this. Students from all racial and social class groupings produced significant academic improvement when tutoring children of the same race and status. The vast majority of tutoring programs consisted of one tutor paired with one tutee - few studies had examined the effect of tutoring in larger groups, but what evidence there was suggested this was less likely to be effective. There was evidence that one-to-one tutoring was of greater benefit than an equal amount of instructional time spent in an ordinary classroom situation. Studies had demonstrated the effect of training in terms of subsequently changed tutor behavior.

A review by Goodlad (1979) concluded that training tutors improved their effectiveness, and that more structured forms of tutoring appeared to yield the best measured outcomes. It was noted that while participants in unstructured tutoring schemes might have favorable subjective impressions of the effectiveness of what they were doing, this tended not to be supported by objective evidence.

The largest research review of this period was that of Sharpley and Sharpley (1981), which deserves to be more widely known. These authors scrutinized reports on 82 peer tutor programs, categorizing them according to the characteristics of the participants, the nature of the tutoring process and the adequacy of research designs. They concluded that a very broad range of students could benefit from the tutoring experience. Low achievers in reading, poorly motivated students, and high achieving students had been able to benefit either academically, socially or cognitively from participation in tutoring programs, as either a tutor or a tutee.

Sharpley and Sharpley concluded that same-age tutors could be as effective as cross-age tutors. The relative ability differential between the tutor and tutee was of greater significance than chronological age or the attainment level of either partner independently. Children tended to prefer a partner of the same gender, but there was no evidence that cross-gender matching reduced attainment gains. Male tutees tended to benefit more from tutoring than female tutees.

Duration of tutoring ranged from ten minutes to 60 minutes a session, and frequency from one session per week to five sessions per week. The median number of sessions per week was three, and the median time 30 minutes. Reading was by far the most frequently researched curriculum area, but others included: mathematics (16 studies), spelling, language skills, social science, foreign languages (French, German, Spanish), grammar and syntax, abstract thinking skills, creative thinking, problem solving, creative and factual writing, and drugs, sexuality and birth control.

In some programs, pre-service training for partners was followed by in-service training. A large majority of studies suggested that tutor training yielded positive outcomes in tutee achievement or tutor behavior. Although unstructured programs using untrained tutors could succeed, they were likely to have a lower success rate. Three experimental studies found no evidence that extrinsic reinforcement produced gains which were superior to non-reinforced groups, while another three studies claimed to have demonstrated that tangible reinforcement did improve the functioning of the tutees, at least on fairly simple tasks in the short term.

Gerber and Kauffman (1981) noted that several studies had compared the effectiveness of peer tutoring to either teacher-led instruction or some form of self-instruction. In general, results indicated that peer tutoring could be at least as effective as teacher-led instruction (under certain conditions), and that tutoring as a supplement to teaching was likely to be better than teaching alone.

In the search for greater objectivity, Cohen, Kulik and Kulik (1982) located more than 500 titles relating to tutoring and carried out a quantitative synthesis or 'meta-analysis' of them. However, only 65 studies fully reported quantitative outcomes for both the tutored and a non-tutored control group, and had no serious methodological flaws. In 45 of 52 studies, tutored students out-performed control students in attainment, while in six studies control students did better and in one study there was no difference (average effect size 0.40).

Larger effect sizes were associated with:

- cross-age tutoring
- structured tutoring
- training for tutors
- tutees of *low* ability
- short-term projects
- mathematics projects
- locally developed tests (c.f. nationally standardized tests)
- published journal papers (c.f. dissertations and other reports).

Tutoring programs had a positive effect on the tutees' attitudes towards the curriculum area being tutored. Seven out of nine studies found the self-concept of tutees improved, but the average effect size was small.

Students who served as tutors performed better than control students in attainment in the tutored curriculum area in 33 out of 38 studies. Four out of five studies found improved tutor attitudes towards the tutored subject, and 12 out of 16 studies found the self-concept of tutors improved.

Overall, Cohen, et al. (1982) concluded: 'These programs have definite and positive effects on the academic performance and attitudes of those who receive tutoring. Tutoring programs also have positive effects on children who serve as tutors, in attitudes and understanding'. However, 'tutoring programs have much smaller effects on the self-concept of children', despite the 'anecdotal reports of dramatic changes' in the literature.

In 1984 Benjamin Bloom reported a series of studies comparing the outcomes of different educational methods. The average student given one-to-one tutoring scored about two standard deviations above the average student receiving conventional classroom instruction. Bloom's description of the search for other methods as effective as tutoring as the "two-sigma problem" subsequently became famous.

Levin, Glass and Meister (1987) conducted a cost-effectiveness analysis of four different interventions to improve reading and mathematics: computer assisted learning, reducing class size, lengthening the school day and cross-age peer tutoring. The best method was four times more cost-effective than the least—it was, of course, peer tutoring.

More Recent Research on Peer Tutoring

Towards the end of the 20th century and into the 21st, research has continued to accumulate and reinforce earlier findings of the effectiveness of peer tutoring. The scope of peer tutoring has continued to widen, particularly with respect to extension to:

- younger tutors
- equal opportunity class-wide programs
- tutors who themselves have special needs
- greater focus on gains for tutors
- other curricular areas
- more complex and challenging content
- same-ability reciprocal tutoring
- materials-free tutoring procedures
- combining tutoring with formative assessment.

It has been known for some years that pre-school children can effectively modify the behavior of siblings and friends (Strain, 1981). An example is the work of Goldstein and Wickstrom (1986) who taught two non-handicapped pre-school children strategies to facilitate interaction during free play in a pre-school facility with three behavior disordered peers. The intervention had immediate effects for all three tutees, and at follow-up there was no regression, despite an abrupt decrease in teacher prompting of the tutors. The authors note that using peers as intervention agents might have a positive impact on the generalization and maintenance of social interaction skills.

A more recent impressive example of peer tutoring with young students is a study reporting the effectiveness of the reading "PALS" program with first-grade tutors and tutees. Findings supported the efficacy of the program for low- and average-performing first graders, and that PALS was not deleterious for the high-achieving (Mathes, Howard, Allen and Fuchs, 1998). This program has been extended to peer tutoring in phonological awareness.

Teachers anxious about embarking upon peer tutoring might be inclined to trust only a small elite group of able students as tutors—perhaps those most like the teacher. However, this approach raises major equal opportunity issues, risks damaging the sociology and ethos of the classroom, and does not begin to capitalize on the full potential of peer tutoring. By contrast, class wide peer tutoring (CWPT) involves everyone.

Positive gains from such programs have been reported by Maheady and Harper (1987) and Maheady, Sacca and Harper (1988). The Juniper Gardens Children's Project (www.lsi.ukans.edu/jg) has developed, promoted and evaluated CWPT for two decades. A recent review of effectiveness research on CWPT from kindergarten to high school by Arreaga-Mayer, Terry and Greenwood (1998) summarizes impact studies in many curricular areas, including with Limited English Proficient students. Cross-age peer tutoring can of course involve the matching of students from each of two whole classes into pairs, although this is somewhat more difficult to schedule. Where certain of the weaker students constantly seem to be in role as tutees, the teacher might arrange for them to visit a lower grade to act as a tutor, to boost their self-esteem.

A number of projects have the primary aim of achieving social and academic benefits for the *tutors*. For example, Custer and Osguthorpe (1983) sought to improve the social acceptance of students with severe learning difficulties by arranging for them to tutor their non-disabled peers in sign language. Following eight weeks of tutoring, interaction between disabled and able pupils was observed to have increased from 5 to 46 percent of available free play time. Sign language tests showed that the disabled students retained an average of 94 percent of the signs they had learned for tutoring purposes during the project, while able students retained an average of 99 percent of the signs they had learned.

Stowitschek, et al. (1982) deployed behavior-disordered adolescents as peer tutors to coach spelling, with immediate and generalized effects. Maher (1982) had conduct problem adolescents act as cross-age tutors for elementary school students with severe learning difficulties. When compared to students in comparison groups who had received alternative 'treatments', the tutors improved significantly on their grades in social science and language arts, and had significantly reduced rates of truancy and disciplinary referrals. These changes were maintained during the follow-up period. Maher, Maher and Thurston (1998) later reviewed several studies with such students, noting many successes but cautioning that some volatility was to be expected.

Scruggs and Mastropieri (1998) reviewed the literature on peer tutoring with special needs students, and concluded:

- Students with special needs benefit academically whether tutees or tutors
- Tutors benefit less academically if there is no cognitive challenge for them
- Participants benefit more if carefully selected and trained
- Participants benefit more if progress is continuously monitored
- Improved attitudes to the curriculum area are frequent
- Improved interactions with partners outside tutoring sessions are frequent
- More generalized attitudinal or interactive gains are less consistent

These findings are very similar to the earlier findings for students without special needs—the differences perhaps being of degree rather than type.

Much early peer tutoring work concentrated on basic skill areas, such as word recognition or oral reading. Consequently, the peer tutoring interaction sometimes contained too much drill and repetition, risking boredom and failing to capitalize on the potential of the method. Recently, there has been much more interest in peer tutoring in more complex and higher order skills, including thinking skills. An early example of this development was Sindelar's (1982) extension into reading comprehension skills using a 'hypothesis-test' tutoring strategy, comparing a teacher-taught group with a peer tutored group. Both groups showed equally large gains. Topping (2001) has further extended this, with the "Paired Reading and Thinking" approach.

Recently, interest has grown in 'reciprocal peer tutoring'—the roles of tutor and tutee alternating in a situation where there is little differential between their abilities. In some cases this has been applied to complex curricular areas, such as reading comprehension. Scruggs and Osguthorpe (1986) had both learning-disabled and behavior-disordered first to sixth graders participate in cross-age tutoring, the special needs students alternating tutor and tutee roles. The participants showed significant gains in reading test scores compared to control groups.

John Fantuzzo and his associates have conducted many studies on reciprocal peer tutoring in same-age, same-ability pairs, using highly structured and supportive classroom materials which help assure quality of error detection and correction. (See Fantuzzo and Ginsburg-Block, 1998, for a recent review, which also discusses linking peer tutoring to parental involvement). The advantages in student self-esteem and social cohesiveness of everyone being able to be a tutor should not be under-estimated.

Many peer tutoring projects do seek to support and scaffold the peer tutoring interaction by having partners work through task cards, worksheets, or other highly structured materials. The production and differentiation of such materials obviously has time and cost implications. Consequently, interest has grown in tutoring procedures in which the interactive behavior is structured, but which can be applied to any curriculum material available.

The 'Pause, Prompt and Praise' reading tutoring technique from New Zealand is a good example, applicable to any reading material within a readability range adapted to the reading competence of the pair (Glynn, 1996). Wheldall and Mettem (1985) deployed eight

16-year-old low-achieving pupils as cross-age tutors for delayed readers aged 12 years. The experimental group made a mean gain of 6 months in reading accuracy, while a group that received untrained tutoring made a mean gain of 2.4 months and a group which had read silently without tutoring made a mean gain of 1.8 months.

Another good example is Paired Reading, applicable to any reading material of the pair's choice provided it is within the independent reading level of the tutor. Topping (1987) summarized outcome data from ten consecutive projects (i.e. unselected and "real world") in one school district. All results were positive, with reading gains for both tutees and tutors – in fact tutors gained more than tutees. The Paired Reading technique has also been used effectively in peer tutoring of adults with literacy problems—by spouses, relatives, work mates, friends and in some cases by their own children, with whom they are in naturalistic everyday contact (Scoble, Topping and Wigglesworth, 1988).

Unfortunately, the term "Paired Reading" has been widely misapplied to almost anything that two people do together with a book, and the specific structured technique has been renamed "Duolog Reading" to emphasize that only this technique has been demonstrated to be effective. Methods of similar effectiveness have been developed in spelling (Cued Spelling) and writing (Paired Writing) (Topping, 1995, 1998a, 2001), and extended to math and science (Topping and Bamford,1998a,b; Topping, 1998b).

A well organized peer tutoring interaction is characterized by regular feedback between the partners, and monitoring and feedback from the managing and supervising professional teacher. This feedback might be enhanced further by incorporating some form of curriculum-based assessment for both tutee and tutor, so they and the teacher can see their progress continuously, and adapt or improve the tutoring process or technique accordingly. Lynn and Doug Fuchs and their colleagues have explored the combination of peer tutoring and curriculum based measurement (CBM) in both reading and math to good effect (e.g., Phillips, Hamlett, Fuchs and Fuchs, 1993). Paired Reading has been combined with computer-based assessment of reading comprehension of real books (Topping, 1997).

Reviews of the effectiveness of peer tutoring continue to be conducted. The most recent at the time of writing (Rohrbeck, Ginsburg-Block, Fantuzzo and Miller, 1999) focused on 81 experimental studies of elementary aged students reported in journals between 1966 and 1998. Evidence continues to accumulate that peer tutoring adds value over and above teacher-led instruction (e.g., Simmons, Fuchs and Fuchs, 1995).

Wider Research on Peer Assisted Learning

As noted in Chapters 1 and 2, peer assisted learning has expanded beyond peer tutoring, and also includes peer modeling, peer monitoring of learning behaviors and peer assessment of learning products. These are newer developments, and not yet so well researched as peer tutoring.

Peer Modeling

Teachers commonly use "cognitive modeling" when demonstrating and explaining through "thinking aloud". Peers can do this also, generally not as well as teachers, but in a way individualized and attuned to the needs of their partner. Modeling combined with verbalization of thoughts has been found more effective than non-verbal modeling alone, perhaps because the learner can repeat the peer model's "think-aloud" to guide their own attempts at independent task replication—in effect a form of self-instruction. Cognitive modeling also often demonstrates strategies and skills, and capable peer models call attention to the repeated crucial common features of their modeling which can and should be generalized to new problems.

Peer modeling also has strong socio-emotional components, since peer models can demonstrate "coping". This is especially important when the learners have difficulties or are encountering a new area of learning. Peer models can demonstrate enthusiasm, motivation and self-belief. They can also credibly illustrate how determined effort can overcome difficulties, not only by their own past and current success but also by their verbalizations during the think-aloud process. By contrast, the flawless and effortless performance of the skilled professional teacher might leave the weak student feeling they are incapable of handling a task that is really easy, with consequent impact on self-confidence. Indeed, there is evidence that peer models can enhance learner self-efficacy more than teacher models, with consequent positive effects on motivation and achievement which generalize to new types of problems (see Schunk, 1998, for a recent review). For the peer models themselves, the act of thoughtful modeling should heighten their metacognitive awareness, and thereby the ability to self-regulate learning.

Peer Monitoring of Learning Behaviors

Class teachers do not have enough time to monitor all children closely. Although peer monitoring requires teacher time for training students, and teachers must continue to invest time to monitor and evaluate it, overall peer monitoring tends to require less teacher time than teacher monitoring.

Feedback from peer monitoring of learning behaviors could enable the learner to better self-regulate their actions toward desired goals. Also, there may be gains for the monitors—practice in checking for off-task behavior in others is likely to sensitize you to off-task behavior in yourself. However, the broader social gains that may occur when students monitor each others' behavior may be as significant as the academic gains.

Many studies of peer monitoring have focused upon its use in relation to inappropriate or problematic social behavior, sometimes in conjunction with self-monitoring. The fewer studies of peer monitoring of learning behaviors have quite often demonstrated effectiveness with students with special needs, such as those with severe and moderate learning difficulties. Peer monitoring can encompass both verbal and non-verbal behaviors. Even students with learning disabilities have been found to be reliable in collecting quantitative peer monitoring data (McCurdy and Shapiro,1992). Reciprocal peer monitoring has also been shown to be effective with students as young as first grade. There is good evidence that the process of monitoring the academic performance of others can improve the monitor's own on-task behavior and academic skills. Monitoring by peers, teachers, and paraprofessionals has been found to be equally effective (see Henington and Skinner, 1998; Brown, Topping, Henington and Skinner, 1999; for recent reviews).

Peer monitoring can serve an assessment function, an intervention function, or both (whether intended or not). Reactivity is a feature of peer-collected data. The process of data collection, even without overt and conscious feedback to its subject, might itself lead to behavior change. However, not least because establishing and strengthening appropriate behavior is generally a more powerful form of learning than requiring students to refrain from inappropriate behaviors, it is usually preferable for peers to monitor and record only positive and appropriate behaviors. Although the process of peer monitoring can bring about change in behavior, and that change tends to be in the desired direction, collecting peer monitoring data may not of itself always be sufficient to create improvement. Teachers should therefore be prepared to implement new interventions or adjust existing ones, using peer monitoring data to evaluate the impact of these changes.

Peer Assessment of Learning Products

Peer assessment by students is now a mainstream idea in colleges and universities (Topping, 1998c), but might seem less familiar in schools. In fact, school teachers have used it for years, perhaps by having students mark or grade each other's tests, or having them evaluate each other's written work prior to teacher assessment. However, peer assessment has much wider potential.

When peers interact to assess one another's work, the purpose is almost always formative. The expectation is that the quality of the work of both assessor and assessed will often improve as a result of the thinking involved and feedback provided. Peer assessment is often reciprocal, members of a pair operating in both roles. Students may improve their skills in critiquing or evaluating their own work (self-assessment) as a result of their interactions during peer assessment (Towler and Broadfoot, 1992). They might acquire new strategies for task performance or fine tune existing strategies. Also, the practice of regulating the activities of others by commenting on the quality of their work might help students internalize techniques for self-regulation (Zimmerman, 1990). When students assess the work of others, they have the opportunity and need to make these processes explicit.

However, the reliability and validity of peer assessment might be less than that of teacher assessment, especially if the assessors are young or inexperienced learners. However, peer feedback is usually available in greater volume and with greater immediacy than teacher feedback, which might compensate for any quality disadvantage. Nevertheless, the provision of clear guidance or assessment criteria and close teacher monitoring and quality assurance are essential. It is also important that the purpose of the assessment is made clear, since if peer assessors think their verdicts have "high stakes" implications, they are likely to err on the side of leniency and abandon any attempt to be creatively critical.

Students might find the idea of peer assessment alarming initially. As peer assessment is often (and should be) a cognitively challenging process, it is unlikely that peer assessors will be able to offer elaborated explanations and justifications for their views during their first experience of it, but this awareness should develop with greater experience and thoughtful scaffolding from the teacher. There is a risk of social contamination—assessments colored by pre-existing social relationships or the desire to form or sustain them. Reciprocity might also foster collusion in giving positive assessments, resulting in a lack of differentiation. Students of different gender have been found to respond differently to peer and adult feedback in different contexts (Dweck and Bush, 1976; Henry, 1979).

A number of studies have demonstrated the benefits of peer involvement in many aspects of the writing process, including improved attitudes. Peer assessment in the form of peer response groups or as a component of peer editing is particularly common. It is also used with classes studying English as a Second Language (ESL) and foreign languages. Many studies of peer editing incorporating peer assessment have not separately measured the effect of the assessment activity from that of the subsequent proposal of corrections. However, several studies have found peer editing to be at least as effective as teacher editing, including in the lower grades and in special education classrooms. A smaller number of studies of peer assessment alone found the same (see O'Donnell and Topping, 1998, for a recent review).

Students often feel that assessment is something that is "done to them"—they have limited understanding of what the parameters of a good performance might be, let alone feel at all in control of them.

Class discussions to formulate consensual criteria for peer assessment can be very enlightening in this regard. Peer assessment gives students a chance to understand the goals of assessment and better direct their performance towards those goals.

Especially in higher education, peer assessment commonly extends to evaluation of presentations, exhibits and portfolios, among other learning products. There is clearly great potential for the wider application of peer assessment in elementary and high schools, as another form of interactive learning with strong implications for student metacognition.

Summary and Conclusions

Teachers might find the following bullet points useful when making a presentation to colleagues:

1. Peer Assisted Learning (PAL) is one of the best evidenced educational methods.
2. PAL costs little and is highly cost-effective.
3. PAL has been used in a very wide range of subject areas.
4. PAL is increasingly used in more conceptually challenging subject areas.
5. PAL usually operates on a one-to-one basis.
6. Commonly, learners (e.g. tutees) gain in:
   - attainment in subject area
   - attitude to subject area
   - social relations with their partner.
7. Commonly, helpers (e.g. tutors) gain in:
   - attainment in subject area
   - attitude to subject area
   - social relations with their partner.
8. More variably, learners *and* helpers gain in:
   - self-esteem, self-confidence, self-belief
   - motivation generally
   - social relations beyond tutoring
   - ability to understand and manage their own learning processes.

9. Gains from being a *helper* have attracted more interest in recent years.
10. Young students (pre-school & K-1) gain—as learners *and* helpers.
11. Special needs students gain—as learners *and* helpers.
12. Ethnic minority and second language students gain—as learners *and* helpers.
13. Males tend to gain more than females.
14. Class-wide PAL is socially inclusive—everyone has an equal opportunity.
15. PAL is at least as effective as equivalent time spent in teacher instruction.
16. Training partners improves effectiveness.
17. More structured programs show higher effectiveness .
18. Cross-age PAL is sometimes more effective than same-age PAL.
19. Cross-age PAL is more difficult to schedule than same-age PAL.
20. Same-age, same-ability reciprocal highly-structured PAL is effective.
21. Cross-gender matching is at least as effective as same-gender matching.
22. PAL without special materials is flexible and effective if structured correctly.
23. PAL combined with curriculum based assessment adds extra value.
24. Extrinsic reinforcement sometimes increases gains, but not reliably.

However, just because peer assisted learning is effective in general, that does not mean it will inevitably be automatically effective right there where you are. Some research studies have failed to produced significant results, and these tend to be rarely discussed or reported. When establishing a PAL project, particularly for the first time, it is essential that it is most carefully organized, and that evaluation is built in.

4

How It Works

Different types of Peer Assisted Learning (PAL) are likely to work in rather different ways. Additionally, the same type of PAL might have its effects in different ways for different pairs, or even for the different students within a pair.

This chapter seeks to give teachers an overview of all the different ways in which PAL might have its effects. This should help teachers when coaching pairs. It should also enable teachers to assess whether the form of PAL in use is really capitalizing on all the possible routes and channels towards effectiveness. If it is not, teachers will wish to fine-tune or develop the PAL to maximize the opportunities for deeper and more extended learning for all participating students.

However, not all of what follows has been exactly demonstrated by research, since it is difficult or impossible to separately measure each of the interacting ways in which PAL is having its effects in any situation. What is offered here is rather a theoretical model of the many possible channels for such effects. This model does have very strong practical implications, however – it is a kind of map for diagnosis and action by the teacher.

First, however, it is valuable to consider the relative advantages and disadvantages of teacher delivered instruction and peer assisted learning. Although they have some similarities, there are also many differences. Teachers need to understand both the similarities and the differences in order to strike the most effective balance between these two complementary methods.

Advantages and Disadvantages of PAL

The relative advantages and disadvantages of teacher-mediated and peer-mediated learning have been explored by a number of writers (e.g., Greenwood, Carta and Kamps, 1990; Maheady, 1998). However, this is something of a false dichotomy, since most Peer Assisted Learning within schools is still engineered, orchestrated, monitored and evaluated by teachers, who are thereby managing the enhancement of learning indirectly rather than directly.

Practice consolidates a skill, promotes fluency and minimizes forgetting. The more you do it, the better you get and the more you want to do it. However, it is important that the practice is positive—i.e. is successful. Well organized Peer Assisted Learning provides a vehicle for supported positive practice of material originally introduced to students directly and perfectly by the teacher.

The advantages of PAL might include more activity, arousal and interactivity than with teacher-delivered instruction, involving considerably more individual attention. This often results in a higher proportion of time engaged with the task—but sometimes also with a higher noise or movement level, which needs managing.

The vocabulary used by peer helpers might be vernacular, simple and more readily accessible than the more professional and complex vocabulary used by teachers. Modeling and demonstration by peers is likely to occur more frequently, be more localized and accessible, and include non-verbal as well as verbal components. Examples given by peers might similarly be more concrete, local, and specific than the more generalized exemplars given by teachers.

The one-to-one attention inherent in PAL facilitates differentiation of the curriculum, giving a greater *quantity* of opportunities to question and to be questioned, although the *quality* of questioning and answering by the peer helper is likely to be significantly poorer than that of a professional teacher.

Students might have lowered anxiety in the peer-assisted learning situation, with correspondingly higher self-disclosure of misconception, error and gaps in knowledge. However, actual detection of such errors, misconceptions and gaps by peer helpers might be much less reliable than that by a teacher. However, peer helpers have more one-to-one contact with their partner than does the teacher, so even though the peer helpers detect a lower *proportion* of errors for a given amount of contact than the teacher, they might detect a higher absolute *number* of errors.

Importantly, when peer helpers do detect errors, they are often able to give feedback to the learner much more immediately than the teacher, which helps prevent the compounding of error upon error. Peer diagnosis of the nature of errors or misconceptions might be low in quality but high in quantity, while the reverse would tend to be true for teachers. The same would be true of the nature of subsequent correction. Prompting opportunities would tend to be high and immediate for peer helpers, but often low and delayed for teachers. The same would be often true for student opportunities to self-correct.

Similarly, opportunities to offer individualized encouragement and praise are likely to be many and immediate for peer helpers, while few and often delayed for teachers. The impact of praise and encouragement from a teacher might be higher than that from a peer, but the potential impact of good quality praise and encouragement from peers should not be under-estimated. Social reinforcement from peers is qualitatively different from that from teachers, and might be equally or more effective (depending on the relationships).

In traditional learning, the student feels accountable and responsible to the teacher. In Peer Assisted Learning, the student feels accountable to both the teacher and their partner. PAL should help to reduce dependency upon the teacher, not least through the proximal and credible modeling of coping by the peer helper (likely to be seen as more attainable than the "expert" performance of the teacher). While teachers always seek to develop strategic metacognitive learning skills, actual practice of these might be more likely within the interaction between peer helper and learner, which should involve personalized cognitive challenge and reflection by both partners, and help develop self-regulation and greater student ownership of the learning process in both.

The balance of time costs requires consideration. Planning and preparation time is needed for any learning activity, but Peer Assisted

Learning has the additional time cost of training peers. Teacher directed learning has much less need for time to be spent on quality assurance and monitoring, but leaves much less time free for such activity. By contrast, Peer Assisted Learning has a higher need for quality assurance and monitoring by the teacher, but frees up the time to enable this to be carried out.

Last, but by no means least, the impact of PAL in terms of personal and social development can be considerable, and for some teachers is more important than any attainment gains. Learning to give and receive praise is important. Teacher exhortations regarding social tolerance tend to be of limited and short-term effect, while learning social tolerance through peer interaction can have more significant and more generalized and durable effects. PAL can certainly impact student social and communication skills even when this is not the prime objective - indeed, perhaps *because* this is not the prime objective. PAL can also have substantial effect on student self-esteem, which can be more generalized than that from direct teacher attempts to raise self-esteem (the latter risking greater dependency and narrower external attributions for success).

Peer Assisted Learning is 'humanly rewarding' (Goodlad, 1979). The helpers learn to be nurturing towards the helped. They develop a sense of pride and accomplishment, and learn trust and responsibility. Many teachers operating Peer Assisted Learning projects find the most striking effect is the increased confidence and sense of adequacy in the helpers. Peer helpers demonstrate or 'model' correct responses for the helped students to imitate, so the PAL process automatically incorporates constant flattering of the sincerest kind for the 'senior partner' of the pair.

Allen (1976) has commented that we live in an 'ageist' society, wherein values and norms are associated increasingly with membership in a broad age category. Little contact occurs between persons disparate in age unless they are members of the same family. Children spend by far the greater proportion of their time with same-age peers — during school time and out of school as well. It has been noted that 12-year-old children spent twice as much time with their age peers as they do with their own parents. At school, the playground may be segregated by age and status, whether officially or unofficially. Cross-age PAL often proves an excellent mechanism for facilitating social interchange and growth within a school.

From the point of view of the helped student, being a 'friend' of a high-status, high-attaining and/or older child is likely to enhance the youngster's self-esteem. Children are extremely important to children, and this may be particularly true as they approach and enter adolescence, and retreat from the influence of parents. The peer helping relationship has few of the institutional and authoritarian overtones of relationships between professional teachers and children—there is no need to maintain a distance. Goodlad (1979) suggests that via PAL projects, students may also gain insights into the processes and difficulties of teaching, which might result in greater respect for their own professional adult teachers.

For the future, in a competitive world, children need to be able to compete. To survive, they also need to be able to cooperate. Johnson and Johnson (1983) compared the effects of competitive, cooperative and individualistic learning experiences on school children. Cooperation resulted in greater positive feelings between children and higher self-esteem and empathy.

Table 1 summarizes these main contrasts between teacher directed and Peer Assisted Learning.

A Model of Peer Assisted Learning

From our consideration of the relative advantages and disadvantages of teacher delivered instruction and Peer Assisted Learning, we can proceed to map the multiple processes and channels through which PAL can have its effects.

The framework initially assigns some of the main sub-processes into one of five categories. The first of these includes organizational or structural features of the learning interaction, such as the need and press inherent in PAL toward increased time on task (t.o.t.) and time engaged with task (t.e.t.), the need for both helper and helped to elaborate goals and plans, the individualization of learning and immediacy of feedback possible, and the sheer excitement and variety of a different kind of learning interaction.

TABLE 1

Teacher-mediated & Peer-mediated Learning: Potential Advantages & Disadvantages

Factor	Teacher	Peer
Engagement		
Activity/Arousal	variable	high
Interactivity	variable	high
Engaged Time	variable	high
Noise Level	low	high
Communication		
Vocabulary of Instruction		vernacular, simple
Modeling/Demonstration	professional, complex	high, also non-verbal
Exemplification	low, mostly verbal generalized	concrete, local, specific
Individualization		
Differentiation	difficult	less difficult
Opportunities to Question	variable to low	high
Opportunities to be Questioned	variable to low	high
Quality of Question/Answer	high	low
Error* Management		
(*misconception, gap, etc)		
Disclosure Threshold	high	low
Detection	reliable, low contact, low f	unreliable, high contact, high f
Diagnosis	high quality, low quantity	low quality, high quantity
Immediacy of Correction	low	high
Nature of Correction	high quality, low quantity	lower quality, high quantity
Prompting Opportunities	low, delayed	high, immediate
Self-Correction Opportunities	low, delayed	high, immediate
Reinforcement		
Encouragement Opportunities	few, often delayed	many, immediate
Praise Opportunities	few, often delayed	many, immediate
Encouragement/Praise Impact	usually high	can be high
Ownership & Metacognition		
Accountability/Responsibility	to teacher	to teacher and peer partner(s)
Dependency on Teacher	higher	lower
Modeling of Coping/Success	by teacher, distant	by peer, proximal
Metacognitive Development	possible	possible for helper & helped
Self-Regulation of Learning	lower	higher
Organization		
Time Costs	planning/preparation	p/p & training
Quality Assurance/Monitoring	lower need, little time available	higher need, more time available
Personal/ Social Development		
Social Tolerance	limited effect	often higher
Social Skills	limited effect	significant effect
Communication Skills	limited effect	significant effect
Self-esteem	variable	higher

Cognitively, PAL involves conflict and challenge (reflecting Piagetian schools of thought, and necessary to loosen blockages formed from old myths and false beliefs). It also involves support and scaffolding from a more competent other, within the Zone of Proximal Development of both parties (reflecting Vygotskian schools of thought, and necessary to balance any damaging excess of challenge). The cognitive demands upon the helper in terms of detecting, diagnosing, correcting and otherwise managing errors and misconceptions is substantial—and herein lies much of the cognitive exercise and benefit for the helper.

PAL also makes heavy demands upon the communication skills of both helper and helped, and in so doing develops those skills. For all participants, they might never have truly grasped a concept until they had to explain it to another, embodying and crystallizing thought into language – another Vygotskian idea, of course. Listening, explaining, questioning, summarizing, speculating and hypothesizing are all valuable skills which should be transferable.

The emotional, attitudinal or affective component of PAL might also prove very powerful. A trusting relationship with a peer who holds no position of authority might facilitate self-disclosure of ignorance and misconception, enabling subsequent diagnosis and correction. Modeling of enthusiasm and competence and the simple possibility of success by the helper can influence the self-confidence of the helped, while a sense of loyalty and accountability to each other might help to keep the pair motivated and on-task.

These five categories of sub-processes feed into a larger onward process. Mechanisms for further development include: adding to and extending current capabilities (accretion), modifying current capabilities (re-tuning), and (in areas of completely new learning or cases of gross misconception or error) rebuilding new understanding (restructuring) (Rumelhart and Norman, 1976, 1983). These are somewhat similar to Piagetian concepts of assimilation and accommodation. Accretion, re-tuning and restructuring extend to the development of each other's declarative knowledge, procedural skill, and conditional and selective application of knowledge and skills.

This leads to the joint construction of a shared understanding between helper and helped—which is adapted to the idiosyncrasies in their perceptions (i.e. is inter-subjective), and is firmly situated within the current authentic context of application, but forms a foundation for further progress.

Subsequently, PAL enables and facilitates further practice, leading to consolidation, fluency and automaticity of core skills. Much of this might occur implicitly, i.e., without the helper or helped being fully aware of what is happening with them. Simultaneously or subsequently, PAL can lead to generalization from the specific example through which a concept is learned, extending the ability to apply that concept and its developmental variants to an ever widening range of alternative and varied contexts.

As this occurs, both helper and helped give feedback to each other, implicitly and/or explicitly. Reinforcement might stem from within the partnership or beyond it, by way of verbal and/or non-verbal praise, social acknowledgment and status, official accreditation, or even more tangible reward. However, reinforcement which is indiscriminate or predominantly for effort risks over-weighting the significance of the reinforced concept in the network of understandings of the learner.

As the learning relationship develops, both helper and helped should begin to become more consciously aware of what is happening to them in their learning interaction, and more able to monitor and regulate the effectiveness of their own learning strategies in different contexts.

This development into fully conscious, explicit and strategic metacognition not only promotes more effective onward learning, it should make helper and helped more confident that they can achieve even more, and that their success is the result of their own efforts. These affective and cognitive outcomes feed back into the originating five sub-processes—a continuous iterative process and a virtuous circle. As the PAL relationship develops, the model should continue to apply as the learning moves from the surface level to the strategic and on to the deep level, and from the declarative into the procedural and conditional.

A framework representing the interaction of the groupings of processes is given in Figure 1—hopefully a useful summary for the busy practitioner in a single chart. The flowchart attempts to identify routes for gains for both the helper and the helped, applicable to all PAL methods in all organizational formats.

FIGURE 1
Groups of Processes Influencing Effectiveness

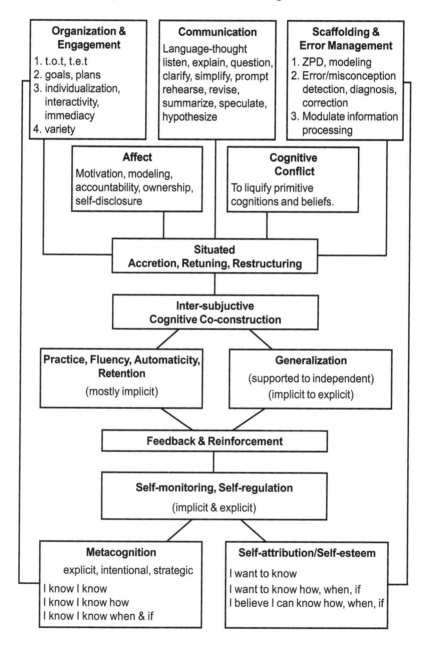

In iterative cycles: Surface → Strategic → Deep
Declaritive → Procedural → Conditional

Implications for Learning and Teaching

The multiple channel process model of Peer Assisted Learning outlined in Figure 1 applies to both helper and helped in different PAL methods in different organizational formats.

Simplistic forms of peer tutoring, focusing on drill and practice, seem likely to utilize only a few of the possible channels or sub-processes (typically only Organization, perhaps some Communication, Scaffolding & Error Management, Practice, and Reinforcement—less than half of the total possibilities). More elaborate and cognitively demanding forms of PAL, such as peer tutoring in thinking skills (e.g., Topping, 2001),

5

Types Of Peer Assisted Learning

In the previous chapter we considered various pathways through which Peer Assisted Learning (PAL) might have its effects. Now we can begin to think about how we might organize it to meet the needs and fit the possibilities of our own particular context.

In this chapter we will review the main organizational dimensions on which PAL can differ, to help teachers select from this "menu" what type of PAL is likely to be most appropriate for their context.

In the two subsequent chapters, we then get down to issues of organization in much more detail.

Peer Assisted Learning can vary on 14 organizational dimensions (at least):

- objectives
- curriculum content
- characteristics of helpers
- characteristics of helped
- method – tutoring, modeling, monitoring, or assessment
- within or between institutions
- within or across year groups
- same or across ability matching
- contact constellations

- fixed or reciprocal roles
- timing
- location
- voluntary or compulsory
- reinforcement

These dimensions are explored in more detail below.

1. Objectives—projects may target intellectual (cognitive) gains, formal academic achievement, affective and attitudinal gains, social and emotional gains, self image and self concept gains, or any combination. Organizational objectives might include reducing dropout, increasing access, etc.

2. Curriculum Content—knowledge or skills or combination to be covered. The scope of Peer Assisted Learning is very wide and projects are reported in the literature in virtually every imaginable subject.

3. Helper Characteristics—the traditional assumption was that helpers should be the "best students" (i.e. those most like the professional teachers). However, very large differentials in ability can prove under-stimulating for the helper, and could inhibit modeling. With lesser ability differentials, all partners should find some challenge in their joint activities. Although the gain of the helped might not be so great, the aggregate gain of both combined may be greater. Many projects have deployed those with learning and behavior difficulties as helpers, to the benefit of the helpers themselves.

4. Characteristics of the Helped—projects may be open to all, or targeted on members of a subgroup, e.g. the especially able or gifted, those with disabilities, those considered at risk of under-achievement, failure or dropout, or those from ethnic and other minorities.

5. Method-choose from peer tutoring, peer modeling of learning behavior, peer monitoring of learning behavior, peer assessment of learning products.

6. Within or Between Institutions—while most Peer Assisted Learning takes place within the same institution, it can also take place between different institutions, as when young people from a high school

tutor in their neighborhood elementary (primary) school, or university students help in regular schools.

7. Year of Study–helpers and helped may be from the same or different years or grades of study.

8. Ability–while many projects operate on a cross-ability basis (even if they are same-year), there is increasing interest in same-ability Peer Assisted Learning. In this, the helper might have superior mastery of only a very small portion of the curriculum. Clear operational structures are necessary to avoid the "pooling of ignorance". Indeed, deficits in "meta-ignorance" can be a problem—the helper might not know that they do not know the correct facts.

9. Contact Constellation–some projects operate with one helper working with a group of peers, but the size of group can vary from two to thirty or more. Sometimes two or more helpers take a group together. More intensive and by far the most usual in schools is Peer Assisted Learning in pairs (dyads)–there is more interpersonal accountability and less opportunity to drift into token participation in a pair.

10. Role Continuity–especially in same-ability projects, role allocation need not be permanently fixed. Structured switching of roles at strategic moments (reciprocal Peer Assisted Learning) can have the advantage of involving greater novelty and a wider boost to self-esteem, in that all participants get to be helpers.

11. Time–PAL might be scheduled in regular class contact time, outside of this, or in a combination of both, depending on the extent to which it is substitutional or supplementary for regular teaching.

12. Place–correspondingly, PAL can vary enormously in location of operation, within and outside of schools.

13. Voluntary or Compulsory–some projects require participation, while in others helpers self-select to participate. This could have marked effects on the quality of what ensues.

14. Reinforcement–some projects involve extrinsic reinforcement for the helpers (and sometimes also the helped), while others rely on intrinsic motivation. Beyond simple social praise, extrinsic reward can take the form of certification, course credit, or more tangible

reinforcement such as edibles or money. Extrinsic reward is much more common in North America than elsewhere, and this has led to some debate about possible excess in this regard. Reassuringly, the research evidence suggests that providing extrinsic reinforcement does not damage intrinsic reinforcement (Cameron & Pierce, 1994). However, its availability can have effects on recruitment in voluntary projects, which might be good or bad.

Readers will see that as PAL can differ in at least two ways on every one of the 14 dimensions, the total number of different types of PAL is very large indeed.

All of the above dimensions along which PAL projects can differ have important implications for organization, which are further explored in the next chapter.

6

Planning and Implementing PAL

There is no doubt that Peer Assisted Learning (PAL) can work. That is unequivocally demonstrated by the research evidence. However, the evidence also shows that Peer Assisted Learning can fail to work, and failure you cannot afford. Careful planning is necessary to ensure that you are successful. This is particularly important if the project is a first venture.

This chapter on planning forms the core of this book. It is very long, but divided into twelve sections which relate exactly to the sections of the Structured Planning Format, which follows in Chapter 7:

A. Context
B. Objectives
C. Curriculum Area
D. Participants
E. Helping Technique
F. Contact
G. Materials
H. Training
I. Process Monitoring
J. Assessment of Students
K. Evaluation
L. Feedback

Much of the guidance given relates to all four PAL methods reviewed in this book: peer tutoring, peer modeling, peer monitoring and peer assessment. Where the guidance for peer modeling, monitoring or assessment is different to that for tutoring, you will usually find the varied or elaborated guidance for modeling, monitoring and assessment at the end of each sub-section, after the guidance for tutoring (particularly in sections D, E and F).

After reading this chapter on planning issues (some sections maybe more than once), you should be in good shape to start planning your own PAL project, using a photocopy of the Structured Planning Format to frame and record your planning decisions.

A. The Context

All children are different, and schools are even more different from each other. All successful Peer Assisted Learning projects have certain common elements, but each must be designed to fit comfortably within the ecology of a particular school at a particular time in its development.

Problems

Careful consideration should be given to potential problems which are specific to your individual establishment. There may be difficulties with massive problems in a particular curriculum area in a particular age group, or with a large proportion of ethnic minority pupils struggling to learn the majority language, or with a high proportion of students with special needs.

Students might be completely unmotivated and have very low expectations of themselves, alienated from the aims of institutional education, and perhaps feeling incapable of playing the part of a helper. There might be an unusually high incidence of off-task and/or attention seeking behavior, linked with a lack of student self-organization and inappropriate or chaotic goal-setting.

The peer group may be divided into sub-groups, with poor relationships between them, and there may be a high incidence of behavior problems in the classroom setting.

If you feel that standards in the school are, in general, lower than they should be, take especial care. The facilities, resources and curriculum in the school may be outdated or poorly organized or culturally inappropriate. It is very important that PAL projects are not used to compensate for, and thereby perhaps disguise, fundamental weaknesses in the professional teaching or organizational infrastructure within a school. Schools that have failed to organize many things are unlikely to have any greater success in successfully organizing Peer Assisted Learning.

It is also important that teachers do not see in PAL a means of giving students extra practice under the supervision and control of the professional as an alternative to the more challenging development of involving the natural parents of the children at home. Natural parents acting as helpers at home have great strengths in this role, as well as weaknesses, which are different from those of either peer helpers or professional teachers.

However, if you are somewhat depressed to realize that you have all too many of the problems listed above, do not despair. Peer Assisted Learning is not a fragile methodology which only works in ideal situations where there are no problems. It can be used to address some of these problems. Indeed, in some cases it takes what you thought was a problem and turns it into an opportunity. You do need to be sharply aware of the problems before you start PAL, however, and be thinking about how to compensate for or otherwise handle these issues.

Support

Although it is possible to operate a PAL project in isolation within the confines of your own classroom with helpers and helped from your own class group, some support from colleagues inside or outside the school is nevertheless highly desirable to maximize the chances of a successful first project. At the very least, the agreement of the school principal will be essential. If this is a new venture for the school, advice and support from colleagues in other, more experienced, local schools or specialist advisory agencies should be sought.

You may encounter four kinds of response from your professional colleagues towards your proposal. Some may feel that what you are intending is fundamentally wrong, and will go out of their way to express disapproval or be more tangibly obstructive. Others will be largely indifferent, but you may be grateful for the fact that they do not actually get in your way. The third kind of response is from those colleagues who express very positive attitudes towards your proposal, thinking it is 'a wonderful idea', and giving you much encouragement. This is all very well, and may make you feel good briefly, but you may find that these positive attitudes are not translated into practical help subsequently. The fourth and most valuable type of response comes from the colleague who is very interested and is prepared to offer you practical help, time and resources, perhaps as part of a learning exercise for themselves.

Throughout your planning, it will be most important that you are very clear about the delegation of any tasks relevant to your project. Where colleagues have agreed to undertake responsibility for specific aspects of organization, this should constitute a cast-iron agreement. You are likely to find it useful to complete the Structured Planning Format (Chapter 7) and circulate copies of it to colleagues who are supporting you so that they are fully aware of the organizational structure of the project—and you may care to indicate their responsibilities with a highlighter.

B. Objectives

You must be clear from the outset as to the objectives of the enterprise. A clear and focused sense of purpose will guide your onward planning, and help prevent you from becoming muddled or over-complicated, and from taking on too much work. Also, clear objectives give a framework for eventual evaluation of the project, and protect you from those who complain that it has not solved every single problem in the school.

Be clear about how your intentions align with the existing curriculum and existing instructional goals and objectives, whether they stem from your own thinking or are prescribed by the principal, your school district, your state or nationally. A PAL project should not be a bolt-on appendage (risking looking like a transient whim or purely a search for novelty)—it should be integrated with your overall pedagogical aims for the year.

Are you aiming for gains in achievement ('academic' attainment or 'cognitive' gains)? Or 'meta-cognitive' gains, so that students show more insight into their own learning processes and thereby become better able to regulate and control them productively? Or motivational gains, so students try harder and appear to value learning more? Or attitudinal gains, in terms of improved attitudes to the curriculum area, or improved attitudes to each other, or improved attitudes towards themselves (in terms of gains in self-esteem and self-confidence and higher expectations)? Or social and behavioral gains, with students becoming more collaborative and less competitive, more on-task and in-seat, more able to work in teams, more able to give and receive praise, more nurturing and less hostile, more cohesive and less alienated?

Which of these are you targeting for the helped students? Which of these are you targeting for the students who are helpers?

Try to specify exactly what you hope to achieve. Try to conjure up a vision of how you wish the students to be doing things differently by the end of the project. Which students, in which curriculum area? What do you see? Write it down in observable, operational terms.

How might these changes be measured? If your objectives are framed only in very vague general terms (e.g. "improved classroom atmosphere"), how will you know if they have or have not been achieved? What exactly would you expect to see and hear which would be good evidence that the "classroom atmosphere" had indeed "improved"?

Different teachers will run peer helper projects for very different purposes, and a success for one teacher could be construed as a failure by another teacher with different objectives and expectations. Objectives do need to be realistic. Do not be over-ambitious, or you will just build in failure for yourself.

It might be reasonable to expect both helpers and helped to show increased competence in the curriculum area of the peer helping, and perhaps increased confidence and interest in that area. However, it is not reasonable to expect a brief project to make a major impact on a longstanding and widespread problem in the school. A degree of reasonable caution when setting objectives creates the possibility of being pleasantly surprised subsequently.

Also remember that your objectives might be quite different from the (unspoken) objectives of the students, at least at the start. They might just be seeking entertainment, in which case you had better make sure that your PAL program is enjoyable for the students, until deeper and more intrinsic motivation kicks in. Sometimes students have quite bizarre ideas about what Peer Assisted Learning might be, which can interfere in a troublesome way until they are unlearned, so take the time to explore their existing pre-conceptions and resistances with your students. Student acceptance and ownership is likely to be better if students perceive that PAL has been introduced for developmental rather than administrative purposes, and detailed feedback is not directly accessed by authority figures.

C. Curriculum Area

Reading is the most popular curriculum area for the establishment of peer helper projects, and within this there is little doubt that oral reading is the most common aspect. Some projects have focused on word recognition skills or decoding strategies, while others have focused more on holistic and fluent extraction of meaning. A smaller number have concerned themselves with more complex and abstract skills, such as higher order comprehension and other reading and thinking skills, while a few have gone beyond this into the area of peer assisted literary criticism.

The language area also lends itself to PAL, and various aspects have been peer assisted. Some projects have concentrated specifically on expansion of vocabulary and understanding of complex concepts. Others have been designed more naturalistically to increase the volume and quality of continuous receptive and expressive language, often utilizing some form of game format.

A related area of curriculum which merits further attention and expansion generally is that of thinking skills and problem solving strategies. Peer Assisted Learning may present an ideal vehicle for such an expansion. This is an area in which you can be assured that both helper and helped will be unable to tick along on half throttle, since every task will by definition be novel and challenging.

Writing skills have likewise been approached in a variety of ways. There is relatively little reference in the literature to peer helping in the early stages of handwriting skill, including such aspects as letter formation. However, more holistic but simply structured programs are available in this area for first grade onwards (see Topping, 2001), and this kind of work will be increasingly developed. With students with more developed writing skills, forms of 'peer response', 'peer editing' and 'critical review' have been widely used. These should focus on semantic as well as syntactical aspects of the writing. Although PAL can include peer oversight of punctuation, capitalization and grammar in the context of continuous writing rather than an artificial test situation, an excess of emphasis on such mechanical aspects of the writing process is likely to be joyless and risk neglecting the main purpose of writing. Once students are competent at working together on single items of writing, their attention could productively turn to larger targets, such as whole collections or portfolios of written work.

A closely associated curriculum area is that of spelling. Here again some projects have emphasized drill, with much rote learning and re-checking of word lists. Other projects have concerned themselves more with generalized spelling skills, dealing with phonically regular spelling by the standard phonological strategies and irregular 'sight' words via some sort of mnemonic or rule-oriented approach.

The mathematics area has also been a popular target. Many projects have concerned themselves with fairly routine drill in mathematical facts and operations, but this runs the risk of swiftly becoming boring for both helper and helped. Other projects have sought to apply Peer Assisted Learning principles to much more abstract concept development in the mathematical area, dealing with tasks such as sorting and conservation in young students, involving much discussion and thereby enhancing competence in the 'language of mathematics'.

Many teachers allow and encourage students to "help each other at the computer", but rarely have a clear and systematic procedure for this which maximizes effective learning and guarantees gains for both helper and helped. Information and Communications Technology skills are a core element of the curriculum in the 21st century, much as reading was in previous centuries. However, unless the class teacher has a particular interest or is particularly capable, some of the students are likely to be more skilful than the teacher in this area. PAL principles enable the design of effective means of utilizing the great potential of peers in this area.

Peer Assisted Learning has also been applied to sophisticated areas of the high school curriculum, such as physical science, social science and foreign languages (including French, German and Spanish). In the latter case, the project organizer can again be assured that both helper and helped will be engaged in a highly useful activity, and indeed Peer Assisted Learning may be the only way in which students of foreign languages can have sufficient oral practice in the context of the ordinary classroom. This presents an interesting parallel to the situation with the development of reading skills. The possibilities are endless for application to all areas of the curriculum, and indeed to learning outside of the classroom.

As noted in the previous section, you must be clear about how your plans align with the existing curriculum and existing instructional goals and objectives, be they personal or externally prescribed. A PAL project be integrated with your overall pedagogical aims for the year. It should also integrate with the mainstream or core curriculum in the school as a whole (although if students move from a teacher who uses PAL to one who does not, they tend to ask awkward and thoughtful questions of the latter).

For ease of organization, project organizers may wish to use packaged techniques or kits of materials for a PAL project (particularly their first), but care must be taken that these materials not only do not conflict with the rest of the school curriculum, but also that the peer helper materials support and integrate with the main strands of curricular experience for all children.

Peer Assisted Learning during class time does of course have an opportunity cost—while you are doing PAL you are not doing something else. You should tackle this 'curriculum displacement' issue head on, since if you try to do PAL as an 'extra' while still doing everything else as well, you will go crazy and probably end up doing nothing properly.

PAL in class is one possible *alternative route* to your educational goals for the year. You will rarely do PAL all year, so the "displacement effect" is constrained. Also, PAL often adds extra value, in that it impacts on more than one curriculum area simultaneously. For example, a PAL program might have attainment effects and also social effects, related to both the regular subject area and to the personal and social development or citizenship curriculum. Two interventions for the price (and time) of one!

D. Selection and Matching of Participants

Having considered *what* (curriculum area), we should consider *who* (will be helpers and helped). Basic structural factors should be considered first. Is a cross-institution or cross-building program desirable or feasible, or would the difficulties of synchronizing time-tables and arranging and supervising transport or movement from place to place be just too much? If the helpers are older, mature, and reliable, the latter might not present too much difficulty—but particularly for a first project, you should try to minimize the things which can go wrong.

Even within the same building, PAL between two different classes (whether of the same or different ages/grade levels) can present problems if the class rooms are far apart, or the route between them is complex or replete with other attractions. For a first experiment, PAL within one class over which the innovating teacher has total control certainly has advantages—less to go wrong and no-one else to blame if something does.

Consideration is also needed of whether the PAL will be class-wide on an equal opportunity basis, or whether it will be confined to a selected sub-group. Teachers who are somewhat anxious about launching into a class-wide approach might prefer to start with a selected sub-group, but this should be representative of the whole class rather than some elite. If you are implementing peer modeling or peer monitoring, you might choose to deploy a small number of helpers working with a large number of students to be helped—perhaps all the other students in the class.

However, you should take great care that you do not give signals that PAL can *only* be done by particular types of student—especially not only by those students who are most like the teacher. Also be careful about signals regarding who it is done *to*, or stigmatization will result. Additionally, it is as well to publicly rationalize starting with a sub-group as a trial or pilot, which will be extended to all students if it proves to be a success.

Class-wide PAL is almost always compulsory, although students typically do not notice its compulsory nature, accepting it naturally as another class activity. In the early stages of a small scale PAL project, you might feel that asking for volunteers would ensure well motivated participants and maximize your chances of success. While this is true up to a point, you need to consider the nature of the group of volunteer helpers—if they are predominantly white middle-class females, the sociological implications and costs of deploying them with ethnic minority socio-economically disadvantaged males needs to be thought through. By sending out the wrong social signals, you might actually reduce the already limited inclination to participate of some students even further. You want PAL to be seen as enjoyable, desirable and 'cool' by all your students before too long.

Background Factors

All teachers have experienced the great variations in general maturity levels shown by classes in succeeding years. It would be particularly unwise to mount a project involving many children where the maturity of the majority to cope with the procedure is in grave doubt. In cases of uncertainty it is usually wisest to start with a small pilot project, to enable further helpers to be added to the project subsequently as a 'privilege'. Where the children have already been used to taking a degree of responsibility for independently guiding their own learning and/or working on cooperative projects in small groups, they may be expected to take to Peer Assisted Learning more readily. You will need to consider these issues for both helpers and helped.

Having said that, Peer Assisted Learning can improve peer group relationships, serve to develop social cohesiveness, and improve work habits. Thus some teachers deliberately deploy it in situations where there is a widespread lack of sharing, cooperation and mutual understanding in a group of children. However, more ambitious operations of this sort are perhaps best left to the more experienced, who have already run successful projects with relatively amenable groups of children.

Age

Remember that an age differential between helpers and helped is probably of less significance in terms of effectiveness than an ability differential. Organizationally, however, students of the same age, grade or year are usually easier to bring together. If you intend to use helpers who are considerably older than the helped, unless you are fortunate enough to teach a vertically grouped or mixed-age class, you are likely to find the organization of the project considerably more complicated, particularly if the helpers are to be 'imported' from another school. Any cross-age helping arrangement will usually create difficulties of matching timetables and movement of pupils.

Although you may find strong views among your colleagues and indeed the children themselves as to the acceptability of either same-age or cross-age PAL, perhaps with strong preference being expressed for one, remember that overall the research suggests that both tend to be equally effective. However, there is some evidence that where the ability (and therefore often the age) of the helper is substantially greater than that of the helped, the helped student may be expected to benefit more, although this may be at the cost of the helper benefiting somewhat less.

Number of Participants

Figure out your target totals of helpers and helped. It is always as well to start with a small number of children in the first instance. Resist any temptation to include 'just one more', or before you know where you are the whole thing will become unmanageable. Particularly for a first venture, it is important to be able to monitor closely a small number of children, and do everything well.

Do not worry about those who have to be 'excluded', provided it is a representative sample of all your students rather than a particular type of student which is socially excluded. They can have a turn later, or be incorporated into the project as your organization of it becomes more fluent, automatic and confident.

Besides, if any evaluation is to be carried out, it will be useful also to check the progress of a comparison group of children who have not (for the time being) been involved in the Peer Assisted Learning.

Contact Constellation

Most Peer Assisted Learning is done in a one-to-one situation, but it can occur in small groups of three, four or five children. For peer tutoring, it is also possible to have two helpers working with a small group of several tutees, but this is more complex and really best done with students already quite sophisticated in PAL methods.

For peer modeling and monitoring, you might choose to appoint only a few helpers initially, to work with all of a small number of students in the class or with all the remaining students in the class. In these circumstances, helping might be reciprocal, or the role might rotate around the class.

For peer assessment, the assessor and assessed student do not necessarily need to be in contact for the actual assessment of the learning product or artifact (e.g. piece of writing), but they do need to be in contact to give the assessment feedback and discuss it. If they are not in contact during the assessment, the assessor will obviously need to make some notes or fill out an assessment schedule in preparation for the ensuing discussion.

Figure out whether you will have pairs or small groups. If you prefer the latter, what size of group? What is the overall ratio of helpers to helped?

If you choose small groups, it is important to make the rules for the group and the specific roles of helpers and helped very clear, or the children may spend more time arguing about organization than actually getting on with the task in hand. You might also find that a small group encourages some students to be 'passengers', leaving the more vigorous and able students to do most of the work—if this is the case, the 'passengers' will gain nothing. It is much more difficult to become disengaged in a pair.

Most of the research on Peer Assisted Learning has been done with pairs rather than small groups, and the former arrangement may prove organizationally more simple, ultimately more satisfying for the 'pairs', and promote a maximum of time on task.

Ability

The range of ability in the children is a critical factor in selection and matching of helpers and helped. When drafting an initial matching on the basis of ability, the names of the available children should be ranked by the teacher in terms of their attainment in the curriculum area of helping. This can be done on the basis of teacher knowledge of the students in the class room situation, or on the basis of recent test results, or on a combination of these, or on any other indicators which the teacher deems reasonably reliable and relevant.

For a cross-ability PAL project between an older and younger class, in which all the older students were helpers and all the younger students were helped, the teachers would produce a ranked list for each class, then pair the top helper with the top student to be helped, and so on down the list. A widely used rule of thumb is to try to keep a differential of about two years in attainment between helpers and helped in such a project.

For a cross-ability project within one class, in the one ranked list draw a line through the middle of the list separating helpers at the top from the helped at the bottom, and then pair the most able helper with the most able helped, and so on.

For a same-ability project (usually within one class, and often involving reciprocal helping), in the one ranked list pair the most able helper at the top of the list with the next most able student who is immediately next on the list, and so on.

Reciprocal PAL is usually done with same-ability pairs, but not always. Some programs deliberately include a component requiring the weaker partner in a cross-ability pair to attempt to help the more able partner (even though the more able partner is unlikely to need it or benefit directly), so that the weaker partner can benefit from the cognitive challenge of helping and it does not all seem one-sided. Other programs have the partners helping each other in somewhat different areas, one partner being strong and a good helper in one area, the other being strong and a good helper in another area. This is often done when working with students with many special needs as well as special strengths, i.e. an uneven profile of skills. Areas of relative competence and strength can be identified with all students, even those with many special needs.

Of course there can be difficulties if the range of ability in helpers and helped is not evenly in parallel, perhaps if an older class of helpers is exceptionally able and those to be helped a particularly poor 'year', or if the spread of attainment in one group is very wide or very narrow or very uneven. Do not worry too much—just match them up as best you can and see what happens—this is not an exact science. Just remember to try to maintain a helper/helped differential which is neither too big nor too small, to maximize the likelihood of gains for both helpers and helped.

In some projects, the alternative approach has been taken of pairing the most able helper with the least able student to be helped, but this creates the situation where the gap in ability is so wide that little stimulation is available for the helper, who is thus unlikely to make attainment gains although probably providing high quality and masterful helping for their partner. This arrangement also leaves students of very similar ability in the middle rankings struggling to help each other, which can look like "the blind leading the blind".

For peer modeling, it is important to select peer models whom students perceive as somewhat similar to themselves in important characteristics. A model who is too disparate from the student to be helped in ability can seem to distant a model to be ever attainable by the student to be helped. Similarity can be based on ability, but also on gender, age, competence, learning style, and the like. If much diversity exists in the class, it is helpful to use multiple models who differ in these attributes. Multiple models allow students to perceive themselves as similar in some respects to at least one model. However, peer modeling usually operates initially on a fixed-role basis, after which the role of model might rotate around the class.

In the absence of ability information, children are more likely to model themselves on same-age peers. When children are able to estimate the ability of peer models, that tends to take precedence over other factors. This seems most important in situations where observers have little information about functional value (i.e., tasks with which students are not familiar or those not immediately followed by consequences).

Peer monitoring can be either cross-ability or same-ability, fixed-role or reciprocal. This is also true of peer assessment.

In peer assessment, some workers have randomly allocated work to be assessed to peer assessors. Arranging same-ability pair matching with reciprocal peer assessment is perhaps the most common, however. This implies matching students with peer assessors they are likely to find credible. Cross-ability matching is less likely to be reciprocal, as the weaker partner would probably have difficulty appreciating the subtleties of the more able partner's work. Project coordinators should reflect on how peer assessors and the students to be assessed should best be matched for their purposes. Contact between assessor and assessed is not essential, as feedback does not have to be verbal and face to face—but most workers assume that this format will yield the greatest benefits.

Relationships

The student's ability is the most important, but by no means the only, factor which must be taken into account. Pre-existing social relationships in the peer group must also be considered.

Obviously it would be undesirable to pair a child with another child with whom there is a pre-existing very poor relationship. However, do not adapt very many of the draft matched pairings on this basis, since part of the value of PAL is to give students a secure framework within which to relate productively. They do not need to learn to relate to peers to whom they can already relate, they need to learn to relate to students with whom they cannot readily relate.

On the other side of the coin, to pair children with their 'best friends' of the moment is unlikely to be a good idea, particularly as the friendship may be of short duration. When children ask "can I work with my friend?", they often mean "can I not-work with my friend?".

Especial care is necessary with the pairings in cases where the helped students are known to be of a particularly timorous or over-dependent personality, or helpers are known to be rather dominant or authoritarian by nature. You can also find this the other way round.

The personality of the helper and the nature of their social relationships and standing in the peer group is important in peer modeling, since the model needs to be salient and significant to the students who are to be helped—they have to regard the model as a person they would aspire to be like in at least some respects. Similarly with peer monitoring and peer assessment—the judgements of the monitor or assessor have to be credible, which will not be the case if they are perceived to be of very low social status or generally incompetent by the students to be helped.

Participant Partner Preference

You might think it desirable to take the individual preferences of the participants themselves into account in some way, and some children might surprise you with the maturity they show in selecting a helper they think would be effective in this role. However, note the point made above about learning to make new relationships. Also consider that to allow completely free student selection of helper is likely to generate a degree of chaos, not least because some helpers will be over-chosen, while others may not be chosen at all, quite apart from the question of maintaining the requisite differential in ability.

One possible compromise is to have the students to be helped express their preferences in writing in a 'secret vote', with each allowed to express up to three choices. In cross-age projects where the potential helpers may be unfamiliar to the helped, some project organizers have had the students to be helped express three preferences based on photographs of the potential helpers. This can make a lot of extra work, however.

The gender balance in the class can present a problem, particularly if there are more girls than boys, since initially some boys (at least in elementary school) express reluctance at the prospect of being helped by a girl. Needless to say, this reluctance often disappears fairly quickly where the teacher allocates a female helper to a male student to be helped and instructs them to get on with it, but the helped student may still have great difficulty justifying what is going on to his friends at recess time. However, one effect of this kind of cross-gender helping may well be to improve relationships and dispel stereotypes.

Many of these social considerations apply equally to the establishment of pairings of mixed race. Peer Assisted Learning can offer a focus for social contact between children who might otherwise be inclined to avoid each other owing to completely unfounded assumptions or anxieties.

Standby Helpers

It is always worthwhile to nominate a 'supply' or 'stand-by' helper or two, to ensure that any absence from school of the usual helper can be covered. Children acting as spare helpers need to be particularly stable, sociable and competent in the curriculum area of the project, since they will have to work with a wide range of students to be helped.

However, do not worry about imposing a burden on the spare helpers, as they may be expected to benefit substantially. In cross-age or cross-institution projects, in which it may be more difficult to ascertain regular and frequent helping contact, more standby helpers may need to be appointed. If there is a danger of any volunteer helpers dropping out before the end of the project, there are again implications for nominating standbys to fill this sort of gap.

Recruiting

Recruiting is of course only necessary if the PAL project is voluntary. The project organizer must decide whether all the class are to be involved, or whether to start with a small group of volunteers and use them as a model of enjoyment which will persuade the rest of the class of the desirability of joining in a little later. There is some advantage in leaving the more diffident children to consider their decision at leisure, since a definite positive commitment will certainly get the project off to a better start. Public demonstration is the most potent form of advertising.

In a project involving same-age PAL within a single class, recruitment will be no problem. At least half of the class will readily volunteer when the nature of the exercise is briefly described. As noted above, your difficulty will be that these are unlikely to be a representative group. You will have to think about how you might stratify this to obtain a representative group.

In cross-age and cross-institution projects, recruitment is always more complex, and publicity more difficult to arrange. Again, it is as well to work in the first instance with well-motivated participants, provided they are reasonably representative. Start small, and as the project progresses momentum should be developed which inevitably draws in other students.

Where helped or helpers do not already exist as a naturalistic group, they may need to be approached individually. In this circumstance, a clear form of words should be prepared which is used consistently in all invitations, to dispel any anxieties which may be aroused by the initial approach. Contact should preferably be made personally, but some project coordinators have utilized written invitations, and publicity by advertisements on posters and handbills, and in newspapers and magazines. The impact of transmission of good news by word of mouth through the 'grapevine' should not be underestimated.

Where peer modeling is in operation, the project coordinator will want to select the first model students carefully, while giving them the option to decline the role—rather different from all-welcome volunteering. This might also be true in peer monitoring, and even in peer assessment, but these are more likely to be deployed on a class-wide basis.

Parental Agreement

The question of parental agreement often arises in connection with peer helper projects. Experience shows that involvement in such a project is usually sufficiently interesting for the students to result in many of them mentioning it at home. This can result in a few parents getting strange ideas about how teachers are using their time (and their students).

It is thus usually desirable for a brief note from school to be taken home by both helpers and helped, explaining the project very simply and reassuring parents that the project will have both academic and social benefits for helpers as well as helped. If a regular home-school newsletter exists, mention of the project there might be sufficient. The necessary minimum of information should be given, couched in a simple and straightforward but reassuring format. (See 'Information for Parents', appended to Chapter 10, which is intended to serve this purpose. It may be photocopied.)

Incentives/Reinforcement

Particularly in North America, some Peer Assisted Learning projects have incorporated some form of payment or tangible reward for helpers, and sometimes tangible rewards for the helped. This is however very unusual in Europe, and there are clearly cultural differences in expectations, quite apart from the question of availability of finance to support this.

The majority of organizers of PAL projects prefer to rely on the intrinsic motivation of helpers and helped alike, using tangible extrinsic reinforcement sparingly, only with students who really need such measures, and then only to engineer an initial 'flying start'.

There is strong evidence that both helpers and helped in a well-organized project not only benefit academically but also develop rewarding social relationships and actually enjoy themselves, so extrinsic tangible reinforcement should be unnecessary.

Some project organizers do utilize badges of identification, certificates of merit and effort, and very small 'prizes' such as pens, but these have much more import at the social psychological level as a token of esteem and an indicator of belonging than as any form of tangible reward.

Social Reinforcement and Modeling

PAL does of course include a great deal of 'social reinforcement' by way of praise, both private and public. Students will differ in their preferences for public vs. private praise. In a group setting, it is also likely to involve 'vicarious reinforcement'—students observing that PAL is visibly socially rewarding for other students, and therefore believing that such rewards can also be gained by themselves.

Teachers should seek to publicly highlight the important components of praiseworthy functional behavior quite specifically, to capitalize on this effect. The progressive introduction of component skills required to perform well, and immediate repeated practice at using these newly acquired skills, will also be important for less able students. Younger and less able children have difficulty attending to modeled events for long periods, distinguishing relevant from irrelevant cues, and organizing information. They are also more easily swayed by immediate consequences of their actions, whereas older and more able students can generally keep longer-term goals in mind and are more likely to perform actions consistent with their goals and values.

Seeing others succeed or fail, or be rewarded or punished, creates outcome expectations, and students are more likely to perform actions when they believe they will be successful or rewarded than when they expect to fail or be punished. However, students' interpretations of reinforcement of others may depend on their confidence and belief in their ability to reproduce the reinforced behaviors. Observing similar peers succeed can raise observers' self-efficacy and motivate them to try the task, because they are apt to believe that if their peers can succeed, they can as well. This is especially true when students are uncertain about their capabilities, are unfamiliar with a (new) task, or have previously experienced difficulties in learning and now doubt whether they can succeed.

Correspondingly, observing similar others fail or have difficulty may lead students to believe they lack the competence to do well, which can lead to avoidance. These considerations may be particularly important for students who have limited histories of receiving reinforcement for appropriate behavior (e.g. behaviorally disordered students).

Students learn new skills and strategies by observing models. Peer models are most influential in situations where perceived similarity to the model provides information about one's own abilities and the appropriateness of behaviors. Observing competent models perform actions that lead to success conveys information about the sequence of actions to use to succeed. Models are informative in another way. Most social situations are structured so that the appropriateness of behaviors depends on such factors as age, gender, or status. By observing modeled behaviors and their consequences, people form outcome expectations about which behaviors are likely to be rewarded or punished, and people's actions are based on their expectations. Of course, some students will lack the ability to identify the important features of modeled acts or the meaning of modeled responses, and this will need scaffolding by the teacher.

The most effective models are thus probably those who are not generally more competent than their observers, but who become competent at performing modeled responses over time. Such peer models are 'proximal' and credible in that they have started where the observer currently is, and model not only current competence, but also step-wise strategies to achieve that level of competence, and (importantly) the socio-emotional aspects of 'coping'. This might be particularly important with students who have a history of learning failures.

E. Technique For Helping

From the outset, you need to decide if your needs, purposes and context are likely to be best served by implementing Peer Tutoring, Modeling, Monitoring or Assessment—in the light of your objectives and the human, material and time resources available.

At an early stage, you also need to decide whether to opt for Fixed or Reciprocal Role PAL, since that engages with decisions about same-ability or cross-ability matching, as well as with decisions about the type of helping technique to be used.

Naturally, the helping technique you choose to use will need to be appropriate for the chronological and developmental age of the target students, both helpers and helped.

Packaged Techniques

There are a number of techniques for Peer Assisted Learning which have been carefully and coherently organized into easily deliverable packages. Examples of these in the reading area include 'Paired Reading' and 'Pause Prompt Praise'. These are designed to be relatively simple albeit structured techniques which are applicable to a wide range of reading materials already available.

With reference to reading comprehension, teachers may wish to experiment with the 'Predict, Question, Summarize and Clarify' technique or 'SQ3R' methods, which are less structured and can apply to any reading material. More complex are the 'PALS Program' and 'Companion Reading', which come with special structured materials and involves the teacher in regular direct instruction prior to each peer assisted session.

Spelling can easily lapse into mindless drill. An interesting variant in the spelling area is the 'packaged' technique known as 'Cued Spelling' (Topping, 1995, 2001).

Another example of a simple packaged procedure is this five-step system to teach impulsive second graders to slow down and thereby make fewer errors:

i.   Cognitive modeling: Model verbalizes while performing the task and child observes.

ii. Overt guidance: Child performs under direction of model's instruction.

iii. Overt self-guidance: Child performs while instructing him- or herself aloud.

iv. Faded overt self-guidance:. Child whispers instructions to self while performing task.

v.   Covert self-instruction: Child performs task while guided by inner silent speech.

There are obviously considerable attractions in using a pre-defined and packaged helping technique, since one may build on the experience of previous workers and avoid unnecessary anxiety about the appropriateness of what one is attempting. Additionally, there will usually be a background of research evidence with which one may compare one's own results. The use of a pre-existing package is thus strongly recommended for those embarking on their first Peer Assisted Learning project. Once experience in the field has been gained, exotic and esoteric new techniques can be the subject of individual experimentation.

General Helping Skills

Peer Tutoring Skills: Some workers have tried to avoid the rigidity sometimes inherent in very highly structured packaged techniques (with or without special materials) by training helpers in more general helping skills. These could include how to present tasks, how to give clear explanations, how to demonstrate tasks and skills, how to prompt or lead pupils into imitating skills, how to check on helped performance, how to give feedback on performance, how to identify consistent patterns of error or problem in responses, and how to develop more intensive remedial procedures for those patterns of error, for instance.

It is obvious that this range of skills is considerably sophisticated. Nevertheless, particularly where relatively able and mature helpers are being used, programs have taken such wide ranging training on board. Various workers have attempted to categorize the requisite skills involved in a number of ways.

Training in ways of giving clear instructions without unnecessary elaboration or the use of difficult vocabulary has been included in some projects. The appropriate point at which to resort to demonstration of the requisite skill may be covered, as may details of how and when prompts should be used. Helpers have been trained in how to give systematic instruction, how to observe responses closely, how to give encouraging but accurate feedback regarding the response, and how to respond differentially to different kinds of student response. Other relevant helper skills have included the identification of areas where the helped student needs extra help, systematic mastery checking, record keeping, the issue of token reinforcement, and the ability to deal with 'take-homes' and home back-up reinforcers.

All of this sounds complicated and ambitious, but care must be taken not to underestimate the abilities of helpers, potential or actual. Many helpers may be well versed in a variety of helping behaviors in other environments, and for many of them training and helping behaviors will merely require the development or shaping of more precise skills from existing repertoires of behavior, rather than instruction from a baseline of no skill at all. However, the demands of this kind of generalist approach are not inconsiderable, both cognitively and socially, and the introduction of such an approach with young or relatively less able children should be left to the experienced Peer Assisted Learning project organizer.

Peer Modeling Skills: Peer Modeling develops the demonstration aspect of PAL in particular, providing not only a competent model which is credible, but also a model of coping which is proximal and therefore encouraging to the observer.

Peer models can also be engaged in supporting learners while they imitate the model (practice the task) and in providing corrective feedback (so the interaction becomes more like tutoring). It helps to accentuate those features of the modeled display to which learners should attend. This can be done through physical means (e.g., distinctive colors), by verbalizing their importance ("watch carefully now"), or by repeating the sequence. Making features distinctive holds student attention, which aids retention. Avoid peer modeling of complex skills, since if models make mistakes, this conveys that the task is hard and will lower feelings of self-efficacy for learning among the observing students.

Consciously modeling coping illustrates how determined effort and positive self-thoughts overcome difficulties. Models initially show difficulty and possibly anxiety, but gradually improve their performance and gain confidence. At first they might verbalize statements of task difficulty and low confidence (e.g., "This is tough," "I don't know if I can do this"), but they then shift to coping statements indicating high effort ("I'll have to work hard"), persistence ("I might be able to do it if I don't give up"), and concentration ("I need to pay attention to what I'm doing"). Eventually their performances improve to mastery level, and their verbalizations reflect confidence, high ability, and positive attitudes. Material should be selected to incorporate a credible degree of difficulty, but not so much difficulty as to produce a high error rate in the model and to prevent them being able to cope with problems and eventually portray the desired behaviors.

Peer Monitoring Skills: It is best to focus on simple target behaviors or events that are easy to observe and record when introducing peer monitoring. As the peer monitors become more experienced, more complex behaviors which correlate more reliably with student achievement can be introduced. For example, peer monitoring might start with checking on whether students appear to be on-task, which is at least readily visible, although not the same thing as time actually engaged with the task.

When behaviors are not easily observed, monitoring of broadly defined observable correlates or related behaviors is possible. For example, although silent reading behaviors are not directly observable, it is possible to determine if a student is on-task (i.e., has head and eyes oriented toward reading material). However, there are many specific behaviors which are readily observable. For example, students can observe if peers have put their name and the date on their assignment, have homework materials ready at the end of the school day, or have erased completely and neatly. While it is time consuming for teachers to monitor these behaviors, peers can quickly check their presence or absence, and cue or prompt when necessary.

Peer monitoring can encompass both verbal and non-verbal behaviors. However, non-verbal behaviors might be interpreted differently by different monitors, and some behaviors are unobservable. However, children can be trained to vocalize or report their inner feelings or emotions and their thoughts as they solve academic problems—a kind of "think-aloud". These verbal reports can then also be monitored by peers. However, the complexity of such reports (and their consequent utility) will vary according to the age, cognitive ability and vocabulary of the subjects. Providing feedback on verbal responses can be useful in other situations. For example, if students verbalize the steps they use in solving a problem, monitors could listen to (observe) those steps, evaluate the steps, and provide corrective feedback. Hopefully the monitor could evaluate whether the peer was likely to leave out steps or make errors before incorrect steps were used in earnest.

Monitoring tasks should be clearly defined and structured. Operational definitions of target behaviors must be clearly explained and supported with numerous positive and negative examples that are relevant to the context in which they will be used. The observational system selected should also be relatively easy for students to master.

Peer monitoring can take different forms, potentially leading to different types of recording: event, frequency, duration, narrative, and time-sample. Event recording requires a monitor to note if (and sometimes when) a specified event (e.g., attainment of a goal) occurs. Frequency recording requires a monitor to keep a tally of the number of observed occurrences of a specified event. Many behaviors are easily counted (e.g., number of problems completed, number of problems completed accurately, number of assignments completed at 80% or better). In duration recording, monitors might be asked to note the amount of time a subject spends responding appropriately (concentration and persistence) before engaging in other behaviors. When narrative recording is employed, monitors provide verbal descriptions of observed events. An example would be to require the peer monitors to write down or audio-record a description of an observed behavior or event which could be considered positive. Partial interval, whole interval, and momentary time sampling procedures allow estimates of time spent engaged in specific behaviors.

Behavioral checklists may also be used to improve monitors' consistency and accuracy. Although peer monitors might initially need teacher assistance and prompting, they should move towards being able to fulfil their role independently.

Because establishing and strengthening appropriate behavior is generally a more powerful form of learning than requiring students to refrain from inappropriate behaviors, it is usually preferable for peers to monitor appropriate behaviors. There might be dangers in peer monitoring of inappropriate behavior, perhaps by drawing attention to these behaviors and increasing the probability of peer rejection. Children might even threaten, physically injure, or socially manipulate another child to prevent them from, or punish them for, reporting inappropriate behaviors. Further, peers may falsely accuse each other in order to cause trouble for another. However, this is arguably less likely in peer monitoring of learning process behaviors than peer monitoring of "high stakes" social behaviors.

Peer Assessment Skills: Peer assessment might be convergent (as in the assessment of whether a student has the correct answer to a mathematics problem), or divergent (as in the assessment of the quality and value of a piece of creative writing). The latter is of course much more demanding. Eapecially initially, participants need a clear explanation and demonstration of just what it is they have to do. What, with whom, where, when, with what materials and why are the key questions needing an answer—not necessarily in that order.

The availability of clear assessment criteria does not guarantee their successful application, which requires transfer from knowledge to skill. Providing effective peer assessment requires a complex battery of cognitive, meta-cognitive, and social skills.

Peer assessment feedback should be descriptive, balanced, specific, and non-judgmental. The skills required depend to some extent on the artefact or product to be assessed and how the assessment feedback is to be given. For example, active participation in face to face peer assessment of writing requires the conscious use of skills in writing, developing and/or applying assessment criteria to written work, and contributing effectively to group discussions. In all circumstances, the assessor must understand the goals of the task, recognize progress towards the goal, judge the potential efficacy of addressing gaps in knowledge or strategy in attaining that goal, and be sensitive to the person to whom feedback is given.

It is also necessary to explicate and enable students to assimilate the problem-solving strategies modeled in peer assessment tasks. Teacher modeling of feedback style and content, and the availability of written prompts, will be needed.

General Social Skills

Because PAL involves interaction, social skills inevitably play a part. Teachers might wish to prepare for the introduction of PAL by introductory work with the class on friendship and its meanings and implications. Any preliminary activities which serve to foster a collaborative ethos among the students should prove useful. Including social "icebreakers" as part of first encounters in training meetings is desirable. This can develop to the greater complexities of establishing rapport, sharing interest, verbal and non-verbal social skills, and so on.

Helping involves a very subtle social process. Some programs take pains to instruct helpers in the establishing of an initial rapport, giving hints on the initiation of conversation, discovering something about the helped and their interests, the importance of revealing things about oneself in order that the helped may do likewise, and so on. It is obviously important for the helper to learn about the interests of the helped in a variety of areas, especially since discovery of a shared interest will do much to cement the bond between the two. In addition to the verbal and non-verbal social skills involved in praising, the importance of aspects of behavior such as physical proximity, eye contact and posture may be incorporated in initial training for helpers.

The attitudes the helper brings to the task are obviously very important, and some workers have dwelt on creating a positive orientation or 'set' to helping in the helpers from the outset. In some programs, helpers have been carefully given a complete overview of the structure of the various components and the aims of the project, to encourage ownership and enhance motivation. The importance of positive attitudes in encouraging regular attendance has been emphasized, and considerable attention given to means of establishing good rapport with helped and stimulating positive motivation in the helped. Sometimes information about the problems of the helped has been given to the helpers in order to develop empathy. Equally, helpers have sometimes been advised about the dangers of feeling too 'sympathetic' towards the helped, and falling too readily into the trap of providing unconscious prompts and excessive help which might foster over-dependence.

Other relevant helper skills have included the ability to manage and refer to any contracts which have been made in respect of the project, and the ability to discuss the progress of the helped with the project organizer or other supervisor, and the helped student themselves.

Criteria

For peer assessment and peer monitoring, the establishment of clear and specific criteria will be necessary, to enable helpers to determine reliably whether a particular student behavior or response or artifact does or does not fall within a particular category. Clearly defined criteria on performance dimensions are likely to better accepted by students, who may well dislike ratings without meaningful scales and generalized ratings directly comparing them to others.

The nature of the criteria will of course vary greatly according to the curricular output to be assessed and the objectives of the exercise. Helpers will always need careful definition and multiple exemplars of application of these criteria. Written prompts or reminders should also be provided. However, teachers must also be alert to the possibility of some students' using written criteria and checklists very rigidly and procedurally, limiting the quality of discourse and providing feedback that is rather sterile.

For example, some teachers advocate the use of "editing sheets" to structure interactions in peer writing response groups. Carefully designed guidelines or question protocols are likely to improve the quality of interaction by prompting elaborated explanations and providing students with an appropriate language to convey their thoughts. In guided cooperative questioning procedures, students develop their own questions about specific topics from generic question "stems" that are designed to promote elaborated cognitive processing, integrating new concepts with relevant previous knowledge.

Teachers will vary the level of structure according to the developmental level and experience of the students involved. For example, inexperienced students could initially be provided with a list of relatively convergent criteria to apply in assessing one another's work (e.g. uses tense appropriately), but subsequently be encouraged to use more divergent criteria and even generate their own criteria from lists of general subheadings.

If helpers have participated in the development of the criteria, they are likely to feel a greater sense of ownership and better motivation. Criteria developed jointly with students are also more likely to be expressed in language which the students can understand.

The opportunity to access a second opinion from another peer assessor or the teacher, and discuss the key features of any assessed artifact on the boundaries of criteria, should always be available.

Drill and Practice vs. Conceptual Challenge

Peer Assisted Learning is undoubtedly valuable for giving students supported and, therefore, largely successful positive practice. However, many of the earlier PAL projects were completely preoccupied with repetitive drill (based on simplistic interpretations of behavioral or precision teaching methods), and arguably failed to capitalize on the many other channels through which Peer Assisted Learning can have its effects. Certainly drill activities are typically summative (preoccupied with the correctness of the final product), rather than formative (concerned with the strategic efficiency and effectiveness of the process of arriving at the product).

When introducing PAL to younger or less able children, an element of routine drill may not be bad to start with, since its simplicity and predictability are likely to boost the confidence of the newly initiated. However, such a focus on surface behavior can rapidly become mechanistic and boring (death by flash card), and does not have the impact of more complex forms of helping technique. A balance between convergent and divergent activity is needed, which is relevant to needs of participants and purpose of PAL project.

Increasingly, PAL methods are being applied to areas of much greater and more complex intellectual challenge, involving more divergent thinking.

Combinations of the Above

The categories referred to above are in no way mutually exclusive, and combinations of aspects of these methods may well be desirable and necessary for a successful project.

Correction Procedure

Errors imply failure, and failure creates stress, and stress can produce a negative reaction in the helped, and possibly also in a helper who feels that errors are an indication of incompetence on their part. To avoid irritation, frustration and disharmony in the helping relationship, all PAL tutoring techniques must include some form of pre-specified error correction procedure. These might also be developed as part of the feed-back following peer assessment.

Whatever this is, it needs to be quick, simple and consistently applicable, easy and non-stressful for both children. If in doubt, the standard simple direct instruction model is a good one. This stipulates that whenever the helped makes an error, the helper signals (usually non-verbally) that an error has been made, the location of the error, possibly the type of the error, demonstrates or models the correct response, leads or prompts the helped student to imitate the correct response, checks that the helped student can produce the correct response unaided, and at some later point re-checks that the helped student can still emit the correct response on request.

This kind of error correction framework can be applied to almost any curriculum area and any kind of mistake, and has the advantage of not leaving the helped student to struggle for any significant length of time before support is forthcoming.

The helper might then go on to prompt their partner to offer alternatives, and comment on those alternatives. Very rarely should the helper give their partner the "right" answer—or what they think is the right answer, since this encourages dependence, and might even lead to further error.

Correction procedures might also be specified in peer assessment projects, if helpers were to be encouraged to go beyond merely giving feedback. However, they are not usually specified in peer modeling or monitoring projects.

Master Reference Source

Well engineered PAL techniques support high quality questioning and discussion, and well engineered correction procedures scaffold the quality of correction, but what about scaffolding the *accuracy* of correction?

If you are operating a convergent form of PAL, in which definite "right answers" do exist, you should consider whether the helpers should be able to access those correct answers in some way (e.g., by referring to the correct solutions often given at the back of textbooks of math problems). This is only likely to be possible where the PAL participants are working with materials from a prepared finite pool, to which model answers are available.

Providing some master reference source of correct responses might be particularly necessary in same-ability tutoring, or other forms of PAL in which the helper's mastery of the PAL curriculum area might be in doubt. It might also prove particularly useful during the practice element of initial training for PAL where the practice was done with standardized items for all participants.

For example, in training for peer assessment of writing, when using a standard piece of anonymous writing for practice purposes for all participants, a master reference version could be provided to helpers with all the errors of mechanics highlighted (spelling, punctuation, syntax, etc). However, this should only be done toward the end of the practice session, so helpers could then self-assess their independent level of "accuracy" and competence, and ensure their partner had been given full and proper feedback.

However, this could not be done with the divergent, creative aspects of writing, and risks sending the wrong signal about what aspects of the writing process are the most important. It also increases the probability of the helpers merely "giving" their partner the "right answer", without focusing on processes and strategies for arriving successfully at the right answers in all contexts.

Praise

If well-considered error correction procedures are carefully and consistently deployed by the helpers, much of the aggravation which can arise when non-teachers try to help children with learning will be avoided. However, merely taking the latent heat out of a relationship is not enough if the result is bland neutrality.

We would wish the helpers to go further than this, and specification is needed of the nature, frequency and circumstances for usage of praise in the helping relationship. It is useful to specify some sort of minimum frequency with which praise should be deployed, but even more important to give a clear indication of those circumstances in which it should always be used.

In Paired Reading, for instance, praise is specified as requisite whenever the child correctly reads a long word where the helper expected an error, and whenever the helped self-corrects before the helper intervenes.

Many helpers find that the giving of verbal praise does not come naturally to them, and they may need considerable practice and feedback in this before an adequate level of performance is achieved. In training, the verbal and non-verbal aspects of praise should be emphasized, since the use of routine praise words in a boring monotone will not have the desired effect. In addition, in some helping relationships the use of a pat on the back or some other gesture may serve to add variety to the social reinforcement.

Some helpers have a very restricted vocabulary of praise words, and part of helper training could include a listing of appropriate vocabulary. In cases of doubt, helpers can be encouraged to discuss this with their helped student, since the latter may be able to generate more culturally appropriate praise vocabulary. In addition to verbal and non-verbal praise, the record keeping inherent in the project organization may include an element of written praise from both helpers and supervising professionals.

Praise is rarely part of peer modeling, and may or may not be incorporated in peer monitoring, but should be a major feature of peer tutoring and peer assessment.

Trouble Shooting

In a first project, particularly when using a self-constructed rather than pre-packaged technique, the project organizer may not be prepared for the sorts of difficulties which arise in helping relationships and the helping process.

Once some experience has been gained, it is worthwhile producing some sort of simple directory of common problems with some indication of how these may be solved. Even if this is not made available in written form to the helpers as a training resource, it will serve as a very handy reference for you. You may rest assured that there will be constant additions to this collection with every subsequent project, for no projects are quite the same and certainly no children are quite the same.

One advantage of using a standard packaged technique for a first project is that clues about likely problems will be found in the literature, together hopefully with some indications of solutions which other people have found effective.

Either way, it will be worthwhile making clear at the outset that problems may arise which are not the fault of either helper or helped. If this is not done, the helper or helped may be inclined when difficulties are first encountered to either blame themselves for the problem or to blame their partner—both of these reactions are highly undesirable.

It is as well for the pair to work on the assumption that if the relationship or process is not working satisfactorily, there is something wrong with the design of the materials or the design of the technique, and they should seek professional advice immediately in order that appropriate adjustments can be made.

As well as communicating this assumption to the helpers and helped, it will be as well for the project coordinator also to make it an essential foundation of their conceptual framework. If the PAL program is not working, it is not the fault of the children, it is because you haven't organized it correctly!

Behavioral Methods

Where a more overtly behavioral method is in use, implying not only detailed checking of task achievement but also the dispensation of tangible or token reinforcement for task achievement, it will be extremely important that the criteria for correct performance are carefully specified.

There is nothing worse than a helped student who feels that their helper is being unduly 'harsh' in their interpretation of what constitutes a correct response. (Where only social reinforcements are on offer, this has much less importance than where tangible and countable indices of success such as tokens are in use.)

Quite apart from the possibility of negative impact on the intrinsic motivation of the helped, heavy use of tangible reinforcement raises questions about the effectiveness of such reinforcement in the long term. The same tangible reinforcer dispensed routinely and massively can produce a saturation effect, and the organizational problems of introducing constant variety may be considerable. The token system is of course intended to get round this problem, but this equally brings its own administrative complexities in relation to the system for exchanging tokens for subsequent tangibles, activities or other treats.

Tokens can of course lead to social rather than tangible (edible, financial) reinforcement. Thus tokens can be exchanged for minutes of off-task conversation or the opportunity to play a game or work on the computer during class time with friends (assuming the friends also have tokens to spend in this way), or perhaps for favored activities (previously available automatically, now available only contingently and when earned).

Tangible reinforcement is rarely part of peer modeling, and may or may not be incorporated in peer monitoring, but is more often a feature of peer tutoring and peer assessment.

Mutual Gain

A final check—even if using a packaged technique, are you sure that the PAL is engineered so that both helpers and helped will benefit? How can you be sure? Take nothing for granted. Does your chosen method maximize use of all available channels for both helper and helped?

Evidential Basis

Another safety check—does your chosen PAL strategy have good empirical evidence on effectiveness? If you have just invented it, make sure that you evaluate it very carefully. If it is a packaged technique, make sure that you can actually locate evidence that it works—beware the packaged techniques which are promoted commercially or by enthusiasts which have no evidential basis, although they might claim to have.

F. Contact

Is PAL contact to be scheduled, or allowed to occur spontaneously as needed? Scheduling is almost always necessary in the early weeks of a project, in order to assure that partners have sufficient regular and frequent practice time to consolidate their PAL skills and that the teacher can be on hand to monitor their performance and give them feedback and extra coaching as needed. Once the teacher is certain that partners are skilful and confident enough to work with much less support and supervision, allowing them to engage in PAL at times of their own choosing becomes possible. Naturally, the nature of contact you choose to allow will need to be appropriate for the chronological and developmental age of the target students, both helpers and helped.

The teacher might choose to launch a PAL project by training everyone together, then schedule PAL time for different sub-groups within the class at different times. This does however require the teacher to be doing PAL monitoring with one sub-group and other activities simultaneously with other sub-groups. There is always the risk that the quality of PAL monitoring will suffer. Consequently, most teachers find it easier to have all their students doing PAL simultaneously.

Peer modeling and peer monitoring are rather different, in that if they are often focused on general learning behavior rather than a specific curriculum area, they might continue throughout the whole day for each day of the week. Indeed, peer monitoring can be operated at times selected at random or with groups of target students to be helped selected at random or purposively in rotation—so the helped students are never sure who is being monitored or when.

When peer monitoring operates, regular review of the monitored outcomes by the teacher will be necessary. Thus, at points in the day determined by the teacher, "review time" can be announced, during which all pairs check on overall progress through the goals of the day. Praise, encouragement and other feedback about progress toward goals can then be offered. With young children, staggered review times for different sets of pairs might be advantageous, to avoid a class-wide "checking frenzy", but this can prove more time-consuming to manage.

With Peer Assessment, designating regular routine peer editing days or sessions might be restrictive, if the teacher does not rigidly schedule the work which is to be assessed for a particular day. Contact between partners is not necessary for assessment to take place, but is necessary for feedback and discussion between them. Partners might instead become familiar with the notion that peer assessment always follows certain activities, whenever those activities occur. However, as with other forms of PAL, regular and closely teacher monitored practice during the first weeks of the project remain essential.

Time

A basic decision is whether the helping is to occur wholly in class time, wholly in the children's recess or break time, or in a combination of both. If the helping is to occur entirely in class time, it can be kept under teacher supervision, but will usually require time-tabling, which may rob the exercise of a degree of spontaneity. If the helping is to occur in the children's recess or break time, some very mature pairs can be left to make their own arrangements, but this is a much greater imposition on helpers and helped alike, and the momentum of the project may begin to peter out as the novelty begins to wear off. Some time-tabling may thus be necessary even during the children's recess or leisure time, so that the size and nature of the commitment involved is visible to all from the outset.

The best arrangement may well be to schedule a basic minimum of contact during class time, but make available the possibility for helping pairs to negotiate further sessions in their own break time according to their own levels of enthusiasm. Some projects have arranged for contact after school, or indeed before school starts in the morning. Such arrangements are of course highly constrained by the transport arrangements for homeward-bound children and should only be attempted if the enthusiasm of the participants is high. Some projects have worked a system of after-school helping, sometimes supported by financial incentives for the helpers, but this is expensive and certainly more complex to organize.

Place

Most Peer Assisted Learning takes place in schools, but it can also be found in libraries, community centers, and other neighborhood locations which are easy of access.

With cross-institution PAL, the transport and movement implications of getting the helpers and helped together will need careful consideration—there is much which can go wrong here. This might also be true for cross-building, cross-campus, or even cross-class PAL.

Finding the physical space to accommodate the pairs can be a problem. In a cross-age helper project within one school, particularly where two full classes are involved, it is possible for half of the pairs to work in the classroom of the helped students and the other half in the helpers' classroom. Finding physical space for the helping to occur during recess or break times may be considerably more difficult if there are problems of recess time supervision and/or children are not allowed access to classrooms.

Clearly, a positive social atmosphere is more likely to be fostered if the children have adequate personal space and are comfortable during their helping. An ambience with a degree of informality is therefore preferable, but the situation should not be so informal as to incorporate many distractions from the helping process. A much used leisure area with heavy passing traffic is therefore unlikely to be satisfactory.

Noise too may be a problem. In Peer Assisted Learning within one classroom, the noise generated by 15 or so pairs of enthusiastic children reading together and engaged in lively discussion can be quite considerable. This is exacerbated in a school with an open internal design, and may generate complaints from other classes who are pursuing a more formal curriculum. It is worth checking the degree of noise transmission in advance, in order to be prepared for this type of complaint.

The availability of an adequate quantity of comfortable seating can also be problematic. Even in a simple reading project, to find enough chairs which may be situated side by side and are reasonably comfortable for both participants might not be easy. Where the Peer Assisted Learning curriculum is more formal and incorporates some paper and pencil work, the availability of tables also has to be considered.

In cross-grade projects, the noise and inconvenience generated by the movement of students from one location to another is also relevant. This is in addition to the other complications of such projects in terms of matching timetables, etc. Seating arrangements need to be such that the mobility of professional supervisors will not be impaired. In cross-institution Peer Assisted Learning, the 'imported' students will need to be briefed about the layout of the building, and shown round—this is, of course, ideally done by other students.

Duration

Each individual helping period should last for a minimum of 15 minutes. Little worthwhile can occur in less time than this, after you have allowed for some lack of punctuality and general settling down. If it is possible for those who so desire to continue for 20 or 30 minutes, this is advantageous. Helping sessions of 30 minutes certainly seem to be the most common period found in the literature. It might be possible for the minimum of 15 minutes to occur just before a natural recess or break time, and there could be provision for the helping pairs continuing into their own recess time if they so desire.

Helping periods as long as 60 minutes are very unusual, and it would be rare for helping to be scheduled as long as this. Peer modeling and monitoring can usually continue for longer than peer tutoring or assessment, since they are generally not so arduous—their effects are also not so immediate. It is always better to leave the helping pair less than exhausted and still a little hungry at the end of their joint experience, in order that they will come to their next session with positive attitudes and high energy levels.

Some pairs will finish their PAL task before the end of the scheduled session, so it is wise to have other activities to hand to keep them productively occupied. If a few students in a class have opted out of a voluntary PAL program, the teacher also has to consider how they are to be engaged in learning individually during the PAL session.

Frequency

To ensure that a project has a significant impact, the frequency of helping contact needs to be at least three times per week, especially in the early weeks when the partners are still developing fluency with the method, and need close monitoring and further coaching. Contact frequency of this order is very commonly found in the literature. However, if four or five weekly contacts can be arranged *and* student motivation can be sustained at this frequency, so much the better. Peer modeling and monitoring are often scheduled every day, at least early in a project. Children involved in peer helper projects rarely object to daily helping, as most of them find it interesting and rewarding. Some pairs may organize their own impromptu sessions in their own recess or break time whether the teacher mandates this or not.

Some projects have incorporated twice daily contacts, but this is rare. Although the literature suggests that the greater the frequency of helping sessions, the more impact a project is likely to have, nevertheless a point of diminishing marginal returns may be found. There is also the problem of finding sufficient time in a very crowded curriculum and school day.

Project Period

The PAL project should be launched with reference to an initial fixed period of commitment. It is useful for both helpers and helped to be clear about what they are letting themselves in for, and how long a course they need to be able to sustain. Additionally, the literature suggests that short-term projects tend to generate bigger effect sizes. Although this may be merely due to capitalization on sheer novelty, teachers are much less inclined than academics to be dismissive about the value of the Hawthorne Effect (the tendency for the introduction of any new form of organization to produce short-term increments in performance).

Apart from the desirability of keeping children hungry for 'a little more', constraints on resources may dictate a short initial experimental period. Particularly in a situation where not all members of a class are involved, there may be a strain on professional staffing in terms of the need to supervise two separate groups of children who in the normal course of events would all be in one classroom under the supervision of one teacher.

So a minimum project period of six weeks is suggested, since it would barely be possible to discern significant impact in less time than this. Popular project periods are eight weeks and ten weeks, which fit comfortably within an average term or semester, and it is not usually desirable to fix a period of longer than twelve weeks for an initial commitment.

It will be much better to review the project at the end of a short initial period, and to obtain feedback from the participants and evaluate the outcomes, and at that stage make conscious joint decisions about improvements or future directions. One thing to definitely avoid is letting the whole thing drift on interminably until it runs out of steam.

G. Materials

Particularly for peer tutoring, learning materials will be necessary. Naturally, the materials you choose to use will need to be appropriate for the chronological and developmental age of the target students, both helpers and helped. These might be special materials which are specific to a 'packaged' program, or they might be regular classroom materials. Occasionally they might be specially made within the school, customized to the requirements of the project, produced by the PAL partners themselves or by other volunteers or by administrative staff under the guidance of the teacher.

Peer modeling, monitoring and assessment have the advantage that they require very little by way of special materials, other than behavioral checklist, a recording form, or a list of criteria.

Structure

In some forms of PAL, highly structured materials are used to guide the interactive behavior of the partners. In other forms of PAL, the emphasis is much more upon training in highly structured but generally applicable interactive behaviors, which can then be applied to any relevant materials which are available.

There is some evidence that Peer Assisted Learning is more effective in raising attainment when structured materials are used than in other circumstances. Certainly, the availability of carefully sequenced materials which take helped student step-by-step, ensuring success along the way, may be easier for helpers to follow reliably and may reduce the need for lengthy and complex training.

However, considerable costs may be involved in the preparation of such materials, or in the purchase of existing structured packages where these are relevant and available. Also, project organizers should beware of the introduction of so much structure that the responses of helper and helped alike become rigid and mechanical. Materials that are too highly structured may inhibit helper initiative and reduce the opportunities for helpers to participate creatively. Complex structured materials might also suffer from automatic inhibition of generalization, in that their restricted availability may prevent additional spontaneous helping from occurring in the project participants' own free time.

Much of the early work in the area showed high effectiveness with structured materials delivered by helpers in a pre-specified and structured manner, but evidence on generalization and maintenance of gains was not always presented. In more recent years, there has been more emphasis on the utilization of structured techniques which specify interactive behavior but are of broad-spectrum applicability to a wide range of materials which need not themselves be structured and are readily available.

Difficulty and Choosing

A related question concerns the control of the difficulty level of the materials. In a very highly structured sequence, some form of placement test may be necessary to determine at what point the helped student should commence. Subsequently, in this situation, mastery of each task determines progression to the next, so the sequence is predetermined, if not the speed of progress.

Other projects have worked on the basis of drafting individual educational plans for each student to be helped, implying pre-specification of a learning sequence for each student, but this is enormously time-consuming.

Other approaches which are less dependent on highly structured materials have allowed some choice by the helped and/or helper from a variety of materials which are nevertheless compressed to be within a band of difficulty. More recently still, techniques have been developed which allow helpers and helped free access to materials controlled in difficulty up to the ceiling level of competence of the *helper*. In these cases, helpers and helped have often been taught skills to enable them to choose mutually interesting materials at an appropriate level of difficulty for both. Choice by negotiation between the pair is the general rule in these circumstances.

However good the training in choosing appropriate materials may be, some of the children in the project will be slow to acquire the requisite skills. This may be because they have lacked practice in this respect in the past, and have become over-dependent on teacher direction. Thus, those members of the project who have not developed the requisite choosing skills after the first two or three weeks of the project may need further gentle encouragement or guidance from the project coordinator.

Some projects have gone further down the road towards independent control of learning by vesting the responsibility for choice entirely with the helped student. (Of course, in all circumstances the difficulty of the material must be controlled to be within the level of the helper's competence.) Unless the teaching of choosing skills is particularly effective, this can result in episodes of inefficient helping, and runs the risk of the helper becoming bored, so some degree of negotiation and compromise is usually seen as desirable—and is of course entirely in the spirit of 'co-operative learning'.

Availability and Sources

Materials are expensive, in cost to buy, in time to arrange loans from resource centers, in time to devise, in time to manufacture and in cost of raw materials. Peer Assisted Learning works by promoting increased time spent on task, and the speed of progress through materials can often be much more rapid than is normal in ordinary classroom teaching. This can create an embarrassment for the project coordinator, who can find the stock of relevant and available materials is rapidly exhausted.

In some circumstances it may be possible for the pairs to make some materials, if not for themselves than perhaps for other pairs, but if this is done the project organizer needs to be satisfied that such joint manufacturing is in itself serving an educational purpose. Carefully structured materials are already available from commercial publishers, but these packages are extremely expensive, and are likely to be beyond the reach of many project organizers, unless they are already available in school and not being used for another purpose, or can be loaned on a short-term basis from a library or other establishment.

A further consideration is the cost of consumables, and some projects involve the consumption of a substantial stock of paper, worksheets etc. Particularly in the area of peer assisted reading, the bringing in to the helping situation of materials gathered by the participants from outside of the school may be possible, and books or magazines may be obtained from participants' homes and local public libraries. Many projects operate on the basis of a collection of paper materials, but if you wish to extend into "electronic" Peer Assisted Learning, the availability of computer hardware and relevant software may be highly desirable.

Access

A school may pride itself on the volume of relevant materials which it possesses, and forget to pay close attention to how easily the pairs can actually access to the material. In reading projects, it is not enough for the school to contain a large number of books, it is also necessary for the children to have very regular and frequent access to them. This is particularly so when the speed of progression through materials is typically much more rapid in the PAL than is expected by teaching staff. It may be logistically easier to mount a special additional collection in some convenient area for access by the pairs.

Project coordinators should also consider the relationship of the project to other school facilities (such as a book shop), the desirability of arranging visits to the local public library, and any other events relevant to the curriculum area of the helping project which can be arranged or are spontaneously occurring.

It is necessary to be clear about which member of the pair takes the initiative on access to materials—is this the job of the helper or helped or both? Do members of pairs need some form of special pass to give them access to otherwise forbidden areas of the school to facilitate easy access to materials? If high status is enjoyed by the helping project (as is usually the case), this kind of free access is seen by the children as a privilege and is very rarely abused.

Progression Criteria

Highly structured materials may have the advantage of inbuilt mastery criteria which make it very clear when the pair are to move on to the next section of the prescribed materials. At the other end of the spectrum, where pairs are allowed a free choice of materials irrespective of difficulty level, as in Paired Reading projects, the issue of progression criterion does not arise, since variability in difficulty level from day to day or week to week is usual, and accommodated by the helping technique.

In the gray area between these two extremes, issues may arise of who determines on the basis of what criteria when the helped student is (a) ready and (b) willing to move on to a fresh set of material, either covering different conceptual content or of more advanced difficulty. The specification of progression criteria will usually be seen by teachers as requiring their professional expertise, but this can be significantly time consuming. Those techniques and materials which have inbuilt progression criteria or have dispensed with the need for progression criteria altogether save the teacher valuable time in this respect.

Recording

It is almost certain that some form of records will be kept of the helping process, if only in terms of progression through materials (e.g. books which have been read by the partners). Given the potentially greatly increased volume of access to these materials, it is essential that the procedures for issuing and tracking materials are highly streamlined, quick and efficient—otherwise a major blockage to the smooth running of the project will ensue.

Recording might be done by the project organizer, some designated assistant such as a librarian or adult volunteer, or by the helpers or the helped themselves, or by some combination of these. Again, some cost is involved in terms of time for preparation, materials used, and time and space for storage and dispensation. There may be official forms constituting record sheets or cards, progress reports to complete, or probes and tests to be accessed at the appropriate moment. Clear specification is necessary of what recording materials are necessary, who is responsible for keeping the records safe and available, who completes them, who obtains them from stock when required, and who replenishes the stock as it is depleted.

Peer modeling, monitoring and assessment require checklists, recording forms, or lists of criteria. If these are individualized, the teacher might be tempted to post the tasks and goals for all children on a single wall chart. However, a (rather dysfunctional) crowd can sometimes gather at this spot. Creating separate individualized charts for each child, pair or group is likely to be more effective, although involving more work.

H. Training

Staff Training

Before teachers set out to train children in particular procedures, it is clearly important that teachers themselves are well versed in the methods to be used. All the relevant professionals need to be fully conversant not only with the technique in use but also the materials, especially where special or structured materials are to be an essential feature of the project.

Even for professional teachers (perhaps especially for professional teachers), there is great danger in assuming that you can learn enough about a technique from written or audio-visual information to be able to train the helpers and helped well. There is no substitute for being taught how to do it yourself by somebody with previous experience, and you will need to have practiced the technique yourself on a child or colleague before trying to disseminate the method further. Actually tackling the tasks that the helpers and helped will be addressing themselves will give you extremely useful insight into the difficulties which they are going to face, and it will certainly not be time wasted. This does mean of course that time has to be found for relevant staff to attend training sessions, with all the implicit difficulties of covering for their classes meantime.

Participant Training: Organization

It is essential that the initial launch of the project at the first training meeting goes well—your project must get off to a flying start rather than fall flat on its face. Training the students individually or in pairs may be highly effective, but would be extremely time consuming and, therefore, not efficient, and most teachers opt to train the participants in groups.

The strong recommendation is to train helpers and helped together from the outset, particularly for peer tutoring or peer assessment. By so doing, you ensure that both helpers and helped receive exactly the same message. In tailoring your training so that the helpers understand it, you will also improve its accessibility to the less able of the helpers. Importantly, training partners together from the start conveys the immediate impression that "we are all in this together", and also serves to avoid any helpers developing delusions of grandeur or superiority.

Even in peer modeling and monitoring, for which training the models or monitors separately might seem tempting, most of the training can usefully involve the children to be helped, since the program should not be clandestine, and indeed is likely to be more effective if all the participants are fully aware of its goals and methods.

Remember that training meetings must always lead on immediately to direct practice of the techniques to be utilized, which is another reason for having helpers and helped together from the start. If in doubt, get them together earlier rather than later.

Venue and Space: You will need to specify well in advance the date, time and place of your training sessions. The number of training sessions, their length and frequency will also need to be made clear to all concerned. This allows the helpers and helped to look forward to their experience and (perhaps) become excited about the impending novel event. It also allows you to make very sure that colleagues are not going to claim the space you intend to use for practice for a last minute play rehearsal or some such.

The physical space in which training is going to occur will probably need the facility for all the participants to sit in a large group and listen to a talk and watch a demonstration, but there will also be a need for chairs (and possibly tables) to be available for subsequent practice, if this is to be incorporated in the same session (rather than taking place back in their regular classrooms). Thus, plenty of seats need to be available and their mobility to fulfil two purposes should be considered. Particularly with oral reading or discussion PAL, remember that noise levels can be a problem, especially in the early stages of training when helpers and helped will not have learnt to modulate their volume.

Materials and Equipment: If audio-visual equipment (e.g. video) is to be used during the training session, try to ensure that you are prepared for Murphy's law to strike at the least opportune moment. The requisite equipment must be: not in use elsewhere, transportable to the location of the training, in good working order and compatible with basic utilities in the training space. Nothing is more distracting or disruptive to efficient learning than having, for example, to wait for an increasingly hysterical teacher to change the bulb in an overhead projector.

The materials to be used for the training session will also need to be readily and reliably available. You may choose to have available for scrutiny the whole range of possible materials, but for the actual practice it will be much better if the specific items and tasks for use by each pair during the practice session have been pre-selected, thus avoiding much student meandering while hunting for an appropriate item.

Even in projects where the helpers or helped are in general to be given a fairly free choice of materials and tasks, paradoxically the training meeting may be the one occasion where you need to control the difficulty level of the materials more rigidly. If, for example, you are using the Paired Reading technique, practice of the Reading Together aspect makes little sense if the helped has chosen a very easy book which he or she is quite capable of reading independently.

Participant Training: Content

Naturally, the training methods you choose to use will need to be appropriate for the chronological and developmental age of the target students, both helpers and helped.

Training might last as little as 30 minutes in total, although somewhat longer is usual. This might be in one block, or spread over a number of shorter step-wise sessions. In peer monitoring, for instance, the amount of training required will depend upon student variables (e.g., level of entry skills), system complexity (e.g., monitoring multiple behaviors versus single behaviors), and the complexity and observability of the behaviors themselves (e.g., in-seat versus using complex problem-solving strategies).

If the helpers and helped have not met previously, you will want to allow time for general introductions, and perhaps some co-operative ice-breaker activity in the working partnerships. Some teachers like to inject humor to relax the atmosphere, perhaps through a "how not to do it" role play by a pair of adults or students from a previous project.

Verbal Instruction: Some teachers tend to over-estimate the impact talking to children (lecturing) has upon subsequent behavior, and this tends to be particularly true of teachers who are used to working with older age groups. Equally, teachers often over-estimate the ease with which children can assimilate information reliably from written materials. In fact, direct verbal instruction and written instruction (in pamphlets or lists of 'dos and don'ts') cannot be assumed to be effective training methods on their own, although they form essential components of any training procedure.

.This issue commonly arises in relation to the use of words like 'tutor' and 'tutee', or 'monitor' and 'monitored', which some project coordinators working with young children prefer to substitute with words like 'helper' and 'helped'. In fact, providing care is taken to clearly define the meaning of the words in advance, their use with even young children can help to give the exercise an air of novelty and heighten its status.

Written Instruction: Written instruction may take the form of continuous prose in a pamphlet, but problems of assimilation may arise for some children. Obviously the readability of the pamphlet should be kept as low as possible, since it is desirable that both helper and helped are able to refer to it subsequently to check anything of which they may be unsure.

However, it may be much more useful to use various forms of checklist, a list of key words or cues, flow charts, diagrams, pictures or cartoons, and so on. For essential reminders about the most important 'rules', class wall posters or individual 'cue cards' may be helpful.

Peer models might such need cue cards. Peer monitors will need recording sheets and brief definitions for reference of the behaviors they are monitoring. Peer assessors will need assessment criteria, possibly definitions of those criteria, and probably some sort of assessment schedule. It is worth remembering the old adage that nobody reads anything which cannot be contained on one side of a piece of paper. People often do not turn over the page.

Demonstration: Having provided verbal and written instruction, it may be worthwhile allowing some time for questions and discussion. However, many of the questions and confusions arising could probably more readily be dealt with by proceeding very rapidly to a demonstration of the required behavior.

This demonstration could be from a videotape available as a standard package from a support agency, or (more convincingly) one made in school. However, there is no need for such sophisticated technology, since it is often possible for the teachers to demonstrate how to use the technique and materials. This could be done with another teacher playing the role of the student to be helped, or with a willing and confident intending or previous helped student.

However, it is much safer to do this with another teacher or volunteer adult, since if they do not give a perfect demonstration (which is highly likely), you will be able to criticize them in front of the helpers and helped in a way which would be problematic with a student actor. Additionally, an adult actor is likely to be more visible and audible to a large group in a training meeting. A video has similar advantages, providing your video replay system is sufficiently large and of adequate quality.

Once a first successful project has been run, experienced helpers and helped can be brought back to demonstrate for subsequent groups of children embarking on the same experience, and this kind of demonstration tends to have the most impact of all. By then, participants should be sufficiently socially robust to be criticized in public, although it is likely that you will plan for some "deliberate mistakes".

In peer monitoring, when learning to discriminate target behaviors on the basis of operational definition, monitors should be provided with examples of behaviors that would and would not qualify. Video can be very useful in this respect.

To demonstrate peer assessment of writing , a sample piece of work can be shown via on overhead (retro) projector, and assessment of its strengths and weaknesses demonstrated by a teacher, who "thinks aloud" through the process and highlights the relevant sections as the assessment proceeds.

Guided Practice And Feedback: Immediate practice of the helping technique is then essential, and feedback should be given from the professionals as soon as possible. In some projects, helpers practice the helping technique by role play on each other before being exposed to the helped, and this may be a useful form of organization if the helping technique is particularly complex. In most cases however, it should be possible to proceed directly to practice in the intended helper/helped pairs.

In peer monitoring projects, before implementing peer monitoring procedures within the target context, peers should be trained to mastery in relevant observation techniques and in the use of program materials to record their observations. For the peer monitoring practice session, pairs can proceed to rate for themselves some further behaviors shown on the video, or in a role play. Much the same applies to peer modeling.

In peer assessment practice sessions, a standard piece of work might be used for all pairs to practice on together (or one of three pieces of work of various complexity, depending on their relative ability), and asked to think aloud, discuss and highlight this anonymous item, before attempting to apply the same principles to a real piece of their own real work. Or you might feel they could cope immediately with applying peer assessment to a real piece of their own work within the practice session. In any event, students should be clear about whether formative feedback from peer assessment is expected to impact their next effort or whether they should rework their current effort.

Checking and Coaching: The behavior of the pairs needs close monitoring during the practice session, and this can put a considerable strain on staffing resources. In a practice session of 20 to 30 minutes, a professional cannot expect to observe in detail the helping technique of more than five or six pairs. Thus if large groups are being trained, a substantial number of 'mastery checkers' who are conversant with the techniques and materials will need to be available—this is undoubtedly the most labor-intensive part of the training procedure.

Those pairs who demonstrate that they have learned the procedures rapidly can be praised and left to continue, but those pairs who are struggling or using deviant technique will need immediate extra individual coaching until they have fully mastered the procedures. Typically, each mastery checker is likely to find that two of the six pairs they are monitoring have learnt the technique extremely well and merely require social reinforcement, another two will have the technique more or less right albeit rather shakily, but are thought to be likely to improve with a little practice, while a further two will be doing something aberrant, and may need to be helped individually through considerable unlearning before a virtual re-teaching of the technique from scratch can occur. Much time will be spent with these last two pairs.

Similarly with peer modeling and monitoring, there is a gradual reduction of teacher prompts and feedback during practice, transfer of the procedure to appropriate classroom activities, and supervision of peer helpers and target students to ensure that the procedure works as intended.

Organization and Contracting: Once the children have been brought to mastery on techniques and materials, they will need briefing about the organizational 'nuts and bolts' of the day to day running of the project. This will include details about access to materials, means of record keeping, arranging times and places for helping contact, and the procedures for further help and follow up (some of these are dealt with in greater detail below). A brief written reminder of these organizational details may be helpful.

Depending on the nature of the PAL project and the maturity and reliability of the helpers and helped, some teachers choose to establish 'contracts' between helpers and helped, or between project coordinators and helpers and helped. If the project is voluntary, some emphasis can be placed on this, with frequent reference to the undesirability of drop-out, together with a little preaching about the significance of the decision to participate. Helpers and helped should decide consciously to be either in the project or out of it, and it should be made clear that half measures will not be acceptable (especially to the peer group).

prove to be surprisingly good at writing positive comments about their partner, and learning to both give and receive praise without embarrassment is a valuable component of PAL projects. By and large, helper comments should be as positive as possible, with any problems discussed directly with the project coordinator via self-referral.

In some cases the helpers soon begin to run out of imagination with respect to their positive comments, and this is an experience which has been shared by teachers who have had to write scores of end-of-year reports. The vocabulary of praise used by helpers can extend much further into the vernacular than a teacher would countenance for themselves, and ideas for praise words can be supplied by the helped student or the comments negotiated between helper and helped, although written down by the helper. Dictionaries of praise words and phrases can be brain-stormed and printed.

The records themselves should be checked each week by the supervising teacher, who can also record some favorable comment and add an official signature, perhaps together with other signs of approval such as points or merit marks for particularly deserving work. The participants will however need to be clear about who is going to check the self-recording, when this is to occur, where the records are to be delivered to, and how frequently this is to be done.

Peer monitoring does of course automatically generate records, and these should be reviewed by the teacher as described above. Peer assessment might generate records in the form of assessment schedules completed by peer assessors. Teachers will wish to develop with their students a policy on whether peer assessors should be allowed (or even encouraged) to write on the work they are assessing in pencil. This often gives the student whose work is being assessed much more detailed feedback than can be contained in an assessment schedule or in a general assessment report, but might be offensive to some helped students, even though the annotations can later be erased.

Discussion

Many projects feature review meetings between coordinating teachers and the helpers and helped. These can occur with the helpers and helped separately or together, and with them in groups or as individuals. The general aim is to discuss how the project is going in general, and any further specific problems.

Group sessions can be valuable for helpers and/or helped to discover that other pairs are having the same problems as they are. On the other hand, individual meetings will elicit more feedback from quiet and shy individuals, but will be much more time consuming. The frequency, duration and nature of such review meetings vary greatly from project to project. Sometimes regular 'planning' or 'de-briefing' meetings have been held between helpers and coordinators. It is probably useful if everybody knows in advance when these are going to occur, but self-referral in the meantime must also be encouraged.

In projects where tokens or other reinforcers are earned for improvement, some coordinators call group meetings to review comparative progress in terms of token acquisition. This can serve to give the whole project a strongly competitive flavor, which could do much to damage the promotion of co-operative learning. The announcement of the gaining of tokens by the group as a whole for the group as a whole may have fewer undesirable side effects.

Direct Observation

Close monitoring and some retraining are likely to be necessary to maintain procedural integrity. For example, deterioration in the use of prescribed error correction procedures is commonly reported in long-term evaluations, and has been directly linked with decline in student learning outcomes.

Of all the monitoring procedures, direct observation is by far the most revealing. Much can be gleaned by the supervising teacher observing individual pairs in rotation. The Peer Assisted Learning session is not an opportunity for the teacher to 'get on with some marking'. On the contrary, the teacher should be circulating round the group observing and guiding children as necessary. In addition, it is possible to ask a particularly expert child helper who is not otherwise engaged to act as an observer in a similar way and report back to the teacher.

A simple checklist of the elements of the technique or other procedure may be useful to help to structure these observations. This could be very similar to, although perhaps a little more elaborate than, the written checklist of 'rules' or 'cues' which could have been given to the PAL pairs as part of the initial training procedure. It is also possible to use video or audio recording for monitoring purposes, and this can be very useful for feedback to individual pairs or the group as a whole, as well as being valuable as a training aid for subsequent projects. However it does take time and expertise to arrange.

With peer modeling, a potential drawback is that peers may model incorrectly. Improper learning can be minimized if teachers carefully select tasks to be modeled such that students can master them with reasonable effort. If peers display incorrect operations, this must be picked up early by monitoring teachers, who can then quickly offer constructive feedback that emphasizes what is correct and what needs reworking. Peer models should not be seen to be struggling in their role, as this can lower the self-efficacy of observers.

Teacher monitoring of peer monitoring is especially important. Peer monitoring can serve an assessment function, an intervention function, or both. Given this assessment function, it is important that the peer monitoring data is accurate and reliable. The behavior(s) being moni-tored, the data recording system, and training may all influence the reliability of peer monitored data.

The reliability and validity of peer monitoring conducted by less able or less mature students might be questionable, so the supervising teacher needs to carry out quality assurance checks, before disputations and argu-ments between monitor and monitored ensue, or more subtle damage is done. Teachers might wish to assign two monitors to one student to be monitored in cases where there is doubt about the reliability of one moni-tor, then compare the two independent ratings (taking care to ensure there is no conferring or copying). If possible, the teacher might undertake some direct monitoring themselves, and compare their own data with those of one or two peer monitors. Alternatively, another adult (whether paid or voluntary) might be recruited to collect such triangulation data.

Much the same applies to the judgements helpers make in the pro-cess of peer assessment. A critical variable requiring close monitoring is the extent to which student errors are actually noticed by the assessor, let alone corrected correctly. This can be an especial concern in ESL or special education classes. Watch out for absent or faulty correction of grammatical errors, reinforcement of errors by peers, and any opportunities for cheating and plagiarism. However, do not underestimate the potential of the peer group itself. You may appoint a particularly capable peer as assistant monitor, but in any event the students will probably learn a good deal from each other spontaneously.

Some teachers choose to conduct their own assessment of a small sample of work that is peer assessed, rotating through the students week by week until all the pairs have been checked in this way. Some teachers assess the peer assessments and give feedback on them to the assessors, while drawing out general points to communicate to all helpers and helped. Where consistency, reliability and validity of helper judgements is found to be shaky, further discussion of and coaching with respect to these issues is clearly needed.

Teachers should expect to fade the strength and frequency of their prompting and monitoring with most students as the project progresses. Do not assume that more able students necessarily need less monitoring, however, since even though surface behavior seems appropriate, this might mask considerable deviance, whether intentional or not. All students will continue to need some monitoring and prompting, although this can usually become more intermittent.

Project Process

Some form of check on basic organizational parameters of the project will also be necessary. The attendance of helpers and helped at scheduled contact times will particularly require monitoring. You may find, for instance, that helping sessions scheduled for the very beginning of the school day are affected by irregularities in public transport, while those which are scheduled for the end of the school day or after school may be rendered problematic at certain times of the year by inclement weather or dark nights. There may be other spontaneous events or acts of God which interfere with the physical space available for helping, or create many distractions to it. If review meetings are to be held between PAL participants and project coordinators, attendance at these and response in them needs to be noted. The availability of appropriate materials will require constant monitoring, as will the frequency and nature of selection and use of these. Organizational problems must be nipped in the bud at the earliest possible moment, and adjustments or modifications introduced as soon as possible.

Recognition of Successful Students

Teachers often choose to celebrate or publicly recognize students during a PAL project. The students recognized will become peer models whether the teacher intends this or not, so the choice of students to be recognized must be informed by this expectation. There are consequently dangers in publicly acknowledging during the course of the PAL activity students who might well have improved in some way but whose performance is still considerably less than perfect. The precise reason or noteworthy aspect of the student's performance which led to the acknowledgement should be specified. In the event of doubt, such recognition should stay a private interaction between the teacher and the students.

Fraud

Teachers should watch for students who have not done what was asked of them and seek to cover this up by inventing or copying data or other evidence of activity. This is rare, but might happen with occasional disaffected students early in the life of a project.

J. Assessment of Students

Some assessment of student progress in terms of learning outcomes is an automatic by-product of teacher process monitoring, especially by direct observation. The teacher will also be checking on student self-recorded evidence of progress through materials, although this might be less reliable as an indicator that learning has definitely taken place. Additionally, the teacher might make informal observations regarding any changes in general learning behavior or learning style, or note any evidence of improved met-cognitive awareness in either helpers or helped students (perhaps by eavesdropping on discussions between pairs).

Peer monitoring can of course serve an assessment function as well as an intervention function. From an assessment perspective, recorded peer monitoring data might have diagnostic value for the teacher. It could provide data on fine grain, high frequency or covert behaviors, or others difficult for the teacher to measure directly. It could provide data enabling the evaluation of other interventions, considering changes from baseline. As noted earlier, given this assessment function, it is important that the peer monitoring data is accurate and reliable. Much the same applies to peer assessment records. You might wish to include a peer assessor self-assessment component—how well can you do peer assessment?—to further promote meta-cognitive development.

Some PAL procedures incorporate peer-administered tests or probes which are integral to helping procedure, as in Cued Spelling, for example. This is a form of peer-administered curriculum based measurement.

However, in order to closely track student progress, the teacher might use some form of regular and frequent curriculum based measurement—generalization tasks, probes, mini-tests delivered and scored by the teacher.

While these might give very accurate, detailed and up-to-date information on the learning progress and current needs of students, they are very time-consuming to administer and score and interpret. Over the last decade, computer programs of increasing sophistication have become available to assist the teacher with the management of information about learning in the classroom. These forms of computerized curriculum based measurement are both delivered to the student and scored by the computer, which then analyzes the results and advises the teacher of the outcome (and sometimes the diagnostic implications for action). They are sometimes termed "Learning Information Systems" (not to be confused with "Integrated Learning Systems", which also seek to incorporate individualized instruction and are much more expensive).

Another relatively recent development is the availability of norm-referenced tests of reading and mathematics which are delivered, scored and interpreted by the computer. Where such tests have a very large item bank, every test presented to every student on every occasion is different, which not only minimizes student cheating but also enables the tests to be taken very frequently without scores being inflated by practice effects as students get to learn the test content. Such tests are of course not as closely tied to the PAL curriculum as curriculum-based tests, but can still form a useful measure of student progress in terms of generalization of skills to novel content.

K. Evaluation

Some form of evaluation will certainly be a feature of your project, even if it is only based on subjective perceptions and general observations.

If you hope to evaluate in a way which gives results of any consistency, reliability or validity, your planning *at the outset* will need to cover this area. To wait until the end of the project before attempting to evaluate is a recipe for confusion and self-deception—all you will be able to check on a post-hoc only basis is whether the 'consumers' say they were satisfied, and whether they have more or less positive attitudes towards their experiences. While this kind of 'evaluation' can give the project organizer a nice warm rosy glow, the 'grateful testimonials' approach will be regarded with cynicism by many hard-headed professionals.

Having said that, to evaluate thoroughly can be fairly time consuming, and there is no point in devoting scarce time to this part of the exercise unless you have particular objectives in mind.

Positive evaluation information can be extremely valuable to feed back in suitable form to the helping participants to enhance even further their motivation. It may also be useful for a wide range of social, educational and quasi-political purposes. Evaluation information can be useful in a host of ways in addition to its primary purpose, which is to check whether what you have done has worked, in order to enable you to adjust or improve your organization on a subsequent occasion. Positive evaluation results can serve to improve the project coordinator's motivation, but if in the final analysis there is no clear purpose in mind, then don't do it, for it is likely to be a waste of time.

The basic principles of designing an evaluation procedure are covered in greater detail later (Chapter 8), but some of the main considerations will briefly be reviewed here.

Firstly, a consideration of the research design is necessary. Most adequate evaluation will include at least a 'before and after' assessment of some sort, hence the need to plan evaluation before the project starts. The school may already routinely collect data in the curriculum area in question, and thus information on progress prior to PAL and after PAL could be readily available. Wherever possible, it is useful to establish a control or comparison group of children who are not experiencing Peer Assisted Learning, or are having some alternative experience which includes as much time on the curriculum task and individual attention as the PAL project.

Attainment and cognitive gains should also be checked in both groups, since the helpers may be expected to gain as much if not more than the helped in these areas. Attitudinal and social gains should be the subject of assessment in both helpers and helped also. Especially in cross-age projects, separate measuring instruments may be necessary for the helpers and helped.

In measuring attainment gains, decisions have to be taken about whether to use some form of norm-referenced testing (to compare progress with normal expectations) or to use some form of criterion-referenced testing (which would check mastery of specific knowledge or information and tasks and skills learned). The latter approach tends to give bigger gains per se, because the assessment is more closely related to what has been learned, but the former gives a better index of generalization to other materials. Some form of assessment delivered and scored by computer (as discussed above) could greatly reduce time costs for the teacher.

Some form of qualitative analysis could be applied, perhaps including error frequency counts, increased speed, and so on. For either norm- or criterion-referenced measurement, a decision will have to be made about whether to assess individually or in a group—this is basically a choice between the quick and easy but unreliable vs. the slow and time consuming but more detailed and trustworthy approach.

The social gains which can accrue from helping will probably be evident from direct observation, but attempts could be made to measure this in other ways, referring to either improved relationships or improved behavior or both. Unfortunately the paper and pencil measures available for this purpose (most typically checklists, rating scales, sociometry and so forth) tend to be of low reliability. The number of disciplinary referrals over time can be counted, but again these tend to be of doubtful reliability. Attitudinal data tends to be equally nebulous. This can come from individual or group interview or discussion, which could be tape recorded for later analysis, or from a variety of questionnaires, rating scales or checklists.

As previously mentioned, the collection of 'process' data about the organizational effectiveness of the project is essential. You will need to note whether:

- training was carried out satisfactorily
- planning and review meetings occurred on time
- planning and review meetings were attended well
- records and other self-report data have been collated, checked & analyzed
- all materials were readily available and used
- the techniques were used properly
- PAL relationships were positive
- mastery was checked as required
- self-referral by either partner was frequent across all pairs
- any 'take-homes' went home regularly & were completed
- any tokens and points were dispensed consistently
- and so on...

Attendance rates, distribution of lengths of helping sessions, information from observational checklists, and so forth can all be analyzed and related to summative outcome information. You might be able to cumulate and synthesize the peer monitoring records or peer assessment records over time, hopefully showing progressive improvement for the majority of students. You might similarly cumulate and synthesize your own informal observations regarding learning behaviors and styles or developments in meta-cognitive awareness. For peer assessment, there might be evidence of improvements in self-assessment in helpers, helped, or both.

Whatever your best efforts, you can be sure that there will be some surprises. Observation may indicate a variety of unpredicted side effects, both positive and negative. You will be interested to see generalization by project students to other times, other materials and other curriculum areas, and from the helping sessions to other students (who may be helped or begin helping spontaneously even though not part of the project). Once you have this kind of motivation and enthusiasm beginning to bubble in the peer group, you will soon begin to think of ways of capitalizing upon it.

Peer Assisted Learning does tend to generate contagious enthusiasm right through an establishment. Generalization from the specific helping curriculum to other wider areas of school life may be evident—thus there may be evidence elsewhere of improved examination results, a higher percentage of academic assignment completion across the curriculum, and so forth.

At this stage, it is easy to be so persuaded by the positive impact of your efforts that you devote all your time to establishing new, grander and more wide ranging PAL projects. A word of caution is necessary. Many educational innovations have shown good short-term impact, but at longer term follow-up the positive results have been found to have 'washed out'. It is thus worth devoting a little of your precious time to both short- and long-term follow-up of social and attainment gains in your original project group.

For the project to have been really worthwhile, some enduring effect should be perceptible six months later, and maybe even twelve months later. How realistic it is to expect one short intervention to have an impact that remains discernible much longer than this is a matter for considerable debate among educational evaluators. In the long run, an accumulation of spontaneous and random events is likely to mask the impact of almost anything.

L. Feedback

The monitoring and evaluation information will need collating and summarizing in some way, or (to be more precise) in two ways. A simple way of presenting the favorable results and information to the participants themselves is necessary to encourage them and promote further growth of confidence. Naturally, the type of feedback you choose to use will need to be appropriate for the chronological and developmental age of the target students, both helpers and helped. A more 'scientific' collation will be necessary to present to interested colleagues, particularly those who will try to pick holes in your report.

It is worth making clear from the outset who is to take responsibility for the collation of information in these various ways, otherwise it might lie around on scraps of paper forever. Decisions must be taken about how to summarize the data for the various purposes, what balance of verbal, numerical and graphic presentation to use, and whether to incorporate any analysis of statistical significance (and if so which).

Feedback to the children can be group or individual, with the helpers and helped separate or together. Do not assume that the children will be easily fobbed off by some vague generalizations from the teacher. They are likely to want something more tangible and structured than that. You must make a decision about whether individual pairs are given information about their own progress (bearing in mind that even if they are not given comparative information they will soon be asking their friends for this), or whether the group as a whole should merely be given information about overall improvement based on group averages.

As evaluation information is given to the participants, it is always useful to make the feedback process reciprocal, and encourage them to give you their views (verbally or in writing or both) on how the project went, and how it could be improved for another generation on a subsequent occasion. Very often the students will make suggestions which are contradictory, and therefore rather difficult to implement, but some of their suggestions will undoubtedly be insightful and extremely helpful when organizing further projects.

At the end of the initial phase of the project, joint decisions have to be made about the future. At this point, the views of the participants must be taken very much into account. Some may wish to continue Peer Assisted Learning with the same frequency, others may wish to continue but with lesser frequency, while a few may be wanting a complete rest at least for a while. When in doubt, a good rule of thumb is to go for the parsimonious option. It will be better to leave some of the children a little 'hungry' and have them pestering you to launch another project in six weeks time, rather than let PAL meander on indefinitely until it quietly expires in a swamp of indifference.

At this point of decision-making, also beware of trying to cater for a wide variety of onward choices from different helping pairs. The organization of the project could become unbelievably complicated if you attempted to accommodate the varying desires for continuation of large numbers of children. It is probably as well to stick with what the majority vote for. Peer Assisted Learning can thus be seen to be not only cooperative but democratic as well.

It might prove equally difficult to identify a significant voting majority for any particular proposed change, whether it be in technique, materials, curriculum area or form of organization. It might also be difficult to obtain a majority view on whether pairings should be changed. Nevertheless, such discussions are useful as an exercise in democracy, language development and organizational problem solving, even if it is the project coordinator who at the end of the day has to make the final decision.

We have noted that most projects have preferred to use the more naturalistic and readily available social reinforcement. You may feel it desirable for those helpers and helped who have completed the initial phase of commitment of your project satisfactorily to receive some form of public commendation for their efforts. Teachers might choose to celebrate those who have made most progress from their own individual baseline, or those who exerted the most effort. Acknowledged gains can of course be in attainment or in the affective or social domain.

Some projects present the children with some tangible tokens of social approval and esteem—certificates of merit or effort, books, badges, pens, and so on. These can be presented in a public gathering in the school, but with older students public praise needs to be used carefully. It is always worth seeking the views of the participants on the nature of any ceremonial. Needless to say, both helpers and helped should be equally eligible for commendation. Some projects have chosen to count a Peer Assisted Learning experience for academic credit, perhaps including the helper's efforts as part of some community service program.

Quite apart from its value as reinforcement for the PAL pairs, some form of public commendation is also useful publicity which may assist in the later recruitment of new helpers.

Reassurance

The danger with any form of instruction is of course that by breaking a naturally acquired skill into its constituent parts, it promotes the 'technicalization' of something which is actually not that difficult. Right now you may well be feeling that the organizing of Peer Assisted Learning is a great deal more difficult and complicated than you had first thought, and you might feel that you have gone off the idea.

Be reassured. Many of the potential problems mentioned above will never come to afflict you. Setting up your first PAL project will undoubtedly be a great deal easier than you imagined. What we have tried to do here is cover all of the possible points of decision.

At many of these points, you can decide the item is irrelevant or decide 'No', and proceed carefully to organize a very simple project, which will probably be very successful. In this case, your completion of the Structured Planning Format (Chapter 7) will be very brief, and the Format will have many blank spaces and be sprinkled with 'No' or 'Not Applicable'.

However, if your project should happen to be less successful than you would have liked, you will be able to review your decisions about organization very easily, and determine where you might have gone wrong or left something out that might have been crucial. Thus, if you don't succeed first time, you will certainly succeed at the second attempt. Now at least you are prepared for anything. Well, almost anything.

7

Structured
Planning Format

This Planning Format should help to inform your initial thinking about your Peer Assisted Learning (PAL) project, help to structure the agenda of subsequent collaborative planning meetings, form a useful record of the planning decisions agreed upon, and enable the consensus decisions to be communicated in a standard form to all the stakeholders.

The Planning Format lists the major questions to ask and areas of decision to consider when planning a Peer Assisted Learning project. You will see that they are laid out under twelve main headings:

A. Context
B. Objectives
C. Curriculum Area
D. Matching Participants
E. Helping Technique
F. Contact
G. Materials
H. Training
I. Process Monitoring
J. Assessment of Students
K. Evaluation
L. Feedback

Do not be alarmed by the apparent size of the Planning Format. It lists many options, only some of which will be relevant to you. The Planning Format strives for a degree of generality which makes it applicable to all sorts of Peer Assisted Learning projects, hopefully without losing too much specificity and practicality.

As and when you make your final decisions, record them on the Format in writing. This will constitute a useful organizational summary to copy and distribute to other interested parties. Inevitably, you will find you need more space under some headings than is actually provided. When photocopying the Format for onward use, enlarge it. Alternatively, scan it so that you have it as an electronic file, then adapt it as you wish.

Some of the sections of the Format are inter-dependent (e.g. D. Selection of Participants and E. Technique of Helping). Thus you might not be able to finalize all your decisions in one linear pass through the Format—you might need to loop back to revisit some sections.

Good luck!

A. Context

1. Problems specific to the situation to be addressed by the PAL project or likely to impair the success of the project?

    a. Low motivation and expectation in students, poor goal-setting?
    b. Low standards of attainment?
    c. Poor on-task behavior, students often seeking teacher attention?
    d. Poor inter-group relationships?
    e. High incidence of behavior problems?
    f. Ethnic minorities, second language, special needs?
    g. Inappropriate accommodation, curriculum, teaching methods?
    h. Other?

2. What supports are available:

    a. from colleagues in school?

    b. from outside agencies and helpers?

3. Who will stand in your way? How will you get around this?

4. Who will give only verbal support?

5. Who will give practical help in time?

6. Who will give practical help in resources?

B. Objectives

1. Specify the objectives of the PAL project:

    a. In observable, operational and preferably measurable terms

    b. In what curriculum area (expanded in section C)

    c. With which students (expanded in section D)

    d. In which of the relevant domains:

        - attainment (cognitive)
        - meta-cognitive (insight into learning processes)
        - attitudinal, motivational (affective)
        - social

2. For the Helpers:
    i.
    ii.
    iii.
    iv.

3. For the Helped:
    i.
    ii.
    iii.
    iv.

4. How does this align with existing instructional goals and objectives?

5. Do you think it is feasible, or is it over-ambitious?

6. Do you think you and your students will enjoy doing it?

C. Curriculum Area

1. Which curriculum areas will your PAL program address?

   a. Reading—oral reading? word recognition? decoding? comprehension?

   b. Language—expressive and/or receptive?

   c. Thinking skills and problem solving.

   d. Writing—creative or technical? single item or portfolio?

   e. Spelling—words or general skills?

   f. Second, other and foreign languages.

   g. Mathematics.

   h. Science.

   i. Information & communication technology skills.

   j. Other (the possibilities are endless):

2. How will this program align with and complement the mainstream curriculum?

3. How might this program conflict with the mainstream curriculum?

4. What will PAL during class time displace?

D. Selection and Matching of Participants

1. Structural factors:

    a. Within or between institutions or buildings?

    b. Within or between classes?

    c. Class-wide or a selected sub-group?

    d. Voluntary or compulsory?

2. Background factors: Current maturity, work habits, cooperative ethos, etc.
    Helpers: Helped:

3. Age: Same-age or cross-age (cross-grade) helpers?

4. Numbers of participants (target totals):
    Helpers: Helped:

5. Contact constellation: Pairs or small groups (of what size?)

    #_____ Helpers per #_____ Helped

6. Ability : Cross-ability or same-ability?
    a. Range of ability in:
        Helpers: Helped:

    b. How do you know this?—what indicators for ranking?

    c. How to maintain a helper/helped differential neither too big nor too small?

    d. Special needs?
       Helpers: Helped:

    e. Special strengths?
       Helpers: Helped:

7. Fixed or reciprocal roles? (see also, Section E—Helping Technique)

8. Relationships

    a. How to accommodate existing positive or negative relationships?

    b. How to accommodate weak and strong personalities?

9. Participant partner preference: Accept to what degree?
    Helpers: Helped:

10. Standby Helpers: Back-up helpers to cover absence/dropout?
    From?   How many?

11. Recruiting (if voluntary): Conducted in person, in writing, advertising, publicity, grapevine?
    Helpers: Helped:

12. Parental Agreement necessary? How much information to give?
    Helpers: Helped:

13. Incentives and reinforcement: Material or other incentives necessary?
    Helpers?   Helped?

E. Helping Techniques

1. Peer Tutoring, Modeling, Monitoring or Assessment?

2. Fixed or reciprocal roles?

3. "Packaged" Technique? (e.g. Paired Reading, Pause Prompt Praise, PALS Program, Companion Study, Predict Question Summarize Clarify or SQ3R, Cued Spelling)

4. General helping skills (e.g. presentation, explanation, modeling, demonstration, prompting, checking, error identification, process monitoring, assessment, feedback, remediation):

5. General social skills (e.g. establishing rapport, sharing interest, verbal and non-verbal social skills):

6. Criteria for peer assessment and monitoring:

7. Drill & Practice vs. Conceptual Challenge: How will you find a balance relevant to needs of participants and purpose of PAL project?

8. Combinations of the above

9. Correction procedure (must be simple and clearly defined):

10. Master reference source of "correct" responses?

11. Praise: Specify frequency of, and circumstances for, praise (must be genuine!):

    a. Verbal:

    b. Non-verbal:

    c. How to avoid criticizing:

12. Trouble-Shooting (what do they do if they hit problems):

13. Behavioral Methods (if used)

    a. Contingencies for correct performance?

    b. What kinds of reinforcement?

14. Mutual gain: Is the PAL engineered so that both Helpers and Helped will benefit? How?

15. Evidential Basis: Does the chosen PAL strategy have good empirical evidence for effectiveness?

F. Contact

1. Scheduled or as-needed? If latter, how will you ensure initial fluency in technique?

2. Whole class simultaneously or rotating groups?

3. Time:

   a. During class time/recess or break time/both/after school?

   b. Times fixed for all or various by negotiation?

4. Place:

   a. At school or other center?

   b. Classroom/leisure or play area/other?

   c. Movement or transport implications

   d. Seating availability and acoustic absorbency (noise!)

5. Duration of sessions: 15, 20, 30, 45, 60 minutes?

6. Frequency: 3, 4, 5, 10 times weekly?

7. Project Period: 6, 8, 10 weeks, 1 semester/term, longer?

8. Logistical problems:

    a. How to match timetables for cross-age/class/institution helping?

    b. How much disruption will student movement create?

9. Other planned activities for students who do not wish to participate or for PAL students who finish early?

G. Materials

1. Origin:

    a. specific to "packaged" program?

    b. regular classroom materials?

    c. specially made materials?

    d. who has time to prepare specially made materials?

2. Structure: Will the program be highly structured and sequenced or flexible and open-ended?

3. Difficulty: Finely graded and of controlled difficulty or teach students how to handle open choice? (NB. Difficulty ceiling must be controlled to helper's level.)

4. Choosing:

    a. Helper or helped to choose, or by negotiation?

    b. Open choice, or open within a specific level?

    c. How much choosing practice before giving guidance?

5. Availability:

    a. Expected financial cost?

    b. Any chance of a loan?

    c. Is expensive hardware required?

    d. Expected cost of consumables?

    e. Can pairs or other volunteers make materials?

6. Sources:

    a. In-house existing materials

    b. Library loan

    c. Special collection

    d. Import from other establishments

    e. Material from participants' homes?

7. Access:

   a. How frequently and easily may students access the materials?

   b. Who takes the initiative on access, helper or helped or other?

8. Progression: Who determines when and how to move to other material?

9. Recording system for loan/possession of materials?

   a. Is it quick and efficient?

   b. Handled by specialist or by helpers/helped?

   c. Who replenishes stock gone missing?

H. Training

1. Staff training: All relevant professionals fully conversant with materials and techniques?

2. Participant Training—Organization

   a. Trained individually or in groups?

   b. Helpers and helped trained separately, together or both?

    c.   Number/length of sessions?

    d.   Venue: date/time/place?

    e.   Audio-visual equipment or other teaching aids: available and working?

    f.   Materials:

- Available, pre-selected?

- Controlled for practice?

    g.   Practice space: check seats and noise levels

3. Participant Training–Content

    a.   Verbal instruction (keep it brief!)

    b.   Written instruction (e.g. pamphlets, checklists, flowcharts, reminders)

    c.   Demonstrations/ role play by teacher, experienced helper or on video

    d.   Guided practice and feedback: Helpers and helped directly, or by role play?

    e. Mastery checking of individual pairs: How many checkers will be available to assist?

    f. Extra coaching for those in need: How many coaches will be available?

4. Organizational briefing (organizational issues, contact, records, etc.)

5. Contracting: In some cases or for all?

I. Process Monitoring

1. Self-referral:

    a. By helper or helped—to whom?

    b. How available is 'expert' help?

    c. What sort/size of problems to be referred?

2. Self-recording:

    a. By helper or helped or both?

    b. For every session or less frequently?

    c. Positive and negative aspects, or just positive?

    d. What criteria and/or vocabulary?

    e. Checking records—who, when, where, how often?

3. Discussion:

    a. Group or individual?

    b. Helpers and helped separate or together?

    c. Frequency and duration of review meetings?

4. Direct observation (by far the most revealing!):

    a. Checklist of criteria/desired behavior to hand?

    b. By project coordinator or spare helper or other?

    c. Video or audio-tape for feedback purposes?

5. Project process:

    a. What checks on organizational aspects?

    b. Frequency/duration of review meetings between professionals?

    c. Need/procedures for minimizing noise or movement levels?

    d. What other adjustment/modifications are needed?

6. Recognition of successful students: Immediate celebration and recognition for following or succeeding with the PAL strategy

7. Need to watch for cheating or other fraud?

J. Formative Assessment of Continuous Student Progress

1. Direct observation by the teacher of learning outcomes.

2. Teacher checks on student self-recorded evidence of progress through materials

3. Teacher checks peer-administered tests or probes integral to helping procedure (peer-administered curriculum based measurement, e.g. Cued Spelling).

4. Teacher curriculum based measurement (generalization tasks, probes, mini-tests delivered and scored by the teacher).

5. Computer assisted curriculum based assessment (delivered or/and scored by computer, e.g. Accelerated Reader).

6. Computer assisted norm-referenced adaptive assessment (assessing generalization, delivered or/and scored by computer, items selected randomly from large item bank on each occasion, can be used frequently without large practice effects, e.g. STAR Reading test)

K. Evaluation (Summative)

1. Purpose of the evaluation (if there's no purpose, don't do it!):

2. Current assessment practice: Extend to give time series data? (i.e. pre-project gains c.f. project gains).

3. Research design:

   a. Pre-post/baseline/comparison group/etc?

   b. Separate measures for helpers and helped?

4. Normative testing:

   a. Standardized tests assessing generalization to compare with 'normal' expectation?

   b. Before and after (pre- and post-test)?

   c. Computer assisted? (delivered or/and scored by computer),

5. Criterion-referenced testing:

   a. Mastery testing to see if specific tasks/skills/information learned (gives better results!).

   b. Error frequency counts, materials mastered, increased speed, etc?

6. Individual vs. group testing:

   a. The quick and unreliable vs. the slow but detailed.

   b. Individual testing on a small sample?

7. Attitudinal data:

   a. From individual or group interview/discussion?

   b. From questionnaires, checklists, ratings?

   c. From other observers' subjective reaction?

8. Social gains:

   a. Improved relations or behavior?

   b. How to measure? (checklists, sociometry, disciplinary referrals?)

9. Self-report data: Analyze and relate to other outcomes.

10. Other process data:

    a. Attendance, mean session length, observation checklists, etc.

    b. Analyze and relate to other outcomes

11. Spin-off:

    a. Observations of unpredicted side effects—positive and negative!

    b. Generalization to other participants, times, materials, subject areas, etc.

    c. Generalization to state or national test or examination results, etc.

12. Follow-up: Short- and long-term follow-up data highly desirable.

L. Feedback

1. Collation of information:

    a. Who will co-ordinates collation process?

    b. How will results be presented for different consumers?

2. Data analysis:

    a. How will data be summarized?

    b. What balance of verbal/numerical/graphic?

    c. Analysis of statistical significance? Educational significance?

3. Feedback to participants:

    a. Group or individual?

    b. Helpers/helped separate or together?

    c. Verbal/written/audio-visual?

4. Feedback from participants:

    a. Group or individual?

    b. Verbal or written?

    c. Suggestions for improvement?

5. Further contracting:

    a. Continue PAL/stop/reduce frequency?

    b. Change PAL method?

    c.   Change PAL technique?

    d.   Change materials?

    e.   Change subject area?

    f.   Change pairings?

    g.   Change organization?

6.   Accolades/Recognition

    a.   Helpers and/or helped?

    b   Public commendation?

    c.   Academic credit?

    d.   Certificates, badges, etc?

8

Evaluating Your PAL Program

Just because spectacular results have been achieved with Peer Assisted Learning in some places, it doesn't guarantee that your program will immediately meet all of your expectations. Especially with your first efforts, you are likely to want to know how successful you have been, with a view to improving effectiveness even more in the future. And evaluating yourself is a lot more comfortable than some outsider doing it. Evaluation will also help convince your colleagues of the value of Peer Assisted Learning, and encourage them to emulate your good work. Beyond that, it may be that your good works will disseminate to other schools, whereby you will indirectly have a profound effect on the education of a very large number of students.

Most importantly, you will find the helpers and helped students very eager to be told how they've done—so you'd better have something concrete to tell them! The helpers and helped will value their own feelings about how well they have done. However, you are the expert, so they will value your opinion on how well they have done even more. If all you have to give them is vague well-meaning platitudes, your credibility (and the program) is going to suffer.

Another major purpose of evaluation is reinforcement for yourself. A fuzzy feeling that the project 'went OK' is unlikely to give you the confidence and reassurance you need to consolidate and develop your Peer Assisted Learning initiative. If you have more concrete data about the success of the project, which is independent of your own subjective views, you will feel you are working from a more solid foundation. Also, if you can present scientific data on your effectiveness as a planner and coordinator of PAL projects, this is unlikely to do your promotion prospects any harm!

One of the great virtues of Peer Assisted Learning is its cost-effectiveness, i.e. what the helpers and helped get out of it for the time and effort put in by professional teachers who are managing and coordinating the project. Thus it would be nonsensical for the professionals to spend a vast amount of their time evaluating a project. However, a small amount of time is probably worth devoting to this task. This chapter details some of the ways of going about it. You will need to choose the ways you think are best and easiest for your own situation.

Measurable Objectives

Before you can determine whether or not your project was a success, you need to be clear about why you did it in the first place. Project coordinators often have a wide range of objectives in mind when they embark on a particular initiative, but they do not always articulate these consciously. Program objectives should be specified at the outset—in a way which is measurable—in clear, precise, observable and operational terms. Don't make this list of objectives unrealistically long or over-ambitious, however, or you will just build in failure. Even with a modest number of objectives, you are unlikely to achieve them all – but you might find there are other serendipitous gains which you had not expected.

Remember that the program objectives espoused by the professional program coordinator may be quite different from those of the helpers, helped, or other relevant professional colleagues. Thus, while you may be out to raise reading attainments, the helped students may be out to have a good time, the helpers may be wanting to feel grandiose and powerful, while the school principal may be wanting the project to reduce conflict in the playground between two sets of pupils, and traditionalist colleagues may be wanting the project to fall apart at the seams to justify their conviction that such modern ideas are doomed to failure and the old ways are undoubtedly the best. Different stake-holders have different objectives, some spoken and some unspoken, and you are most unlikely to be able to meet all of them.

Types of Evaluation

There are two main types of evaluation: 'Process' (or Formative) evaluation and 'Product' (or Summative or Outcome) evaluation. Summation or Outcome evaluation looks solely at the end-product of a project, without looking closely at how effective each of the various aspects of the organization and methods of the project were in achieving this goal. These latter questions are the focus of Formative evaluation, so named because the data gathered enable you to re-form a better project next time, or even adjust the current one as you go along.

A number of reports of projects in the literature include no data about outcomes, but merely constitute a description of how the project worked. This is all very well up to a point, and is an essential aspect of an overall evaluation, but the description itself needs to be precise and have some quantitative aspects. How many meetings were held, and what was the attendance rate by different categories of personnel? What was the participation rate of helpers and helped, as well as frequency and regularity of contacts made during the project? Was the desired behavior demonstrated by helpers, helped and project coordinators? Did the helpers actually implement the helping procedures in which they had been trained, or could the improvement shown by the helped students be attributed solely to the effect of extra individual attention? Did the project coordinator monitor PAL sessions regularly and frequently as expected? Were learning materials prepared in good time and always brought to sessions? Was record keeping completed as required, and were all records subsequently collated for analysis?

The fundamental question with the Process aspect of project evaluation is whether or not the project actually operated as planned and intended. Without process data, outcome data cannot be construed to reflect upon the effectiveness of the program. On the other hand, even a quantitative description of project process remains no more than that—it tells us whether the project was put into operation as intended, but does not tell us whether it 'worked'.

Research Design

Evaluation research is basically about detecting change (and preferably measuring the degree of change). The obvious thing is to apply your measure(s) at the start of the project and again at the end of the project to the students who take part (Pre-Post Test Design). But if your measure is not norm-referenced (standardized), you will have no way of telling whether the children would have made the pre-post changes anyway, irrespective of the project. Even if your measure is norm-referenced (like a standardized reading test), unless your results are spectacularly better than 'normal' rates of gain, you still won't have proof that the children could only have made those gains with the help of the project. Standardization refers to averages for hundreds of children from all over the country.

However, the standardization may not be immediately relevant to a small group of children with peculiar attainment profiles in your particular educational establishment. So you really need to compare the progress of your project students with the progress of a similar local group who have not been involved in the project. If you offer involvement in the project to 20 students, but only ten finally participate, you can use the ten 'drop-outs' as a 'comparison' group.

But the ten drop-outs are not a true 'control' group, because they have self-selected not to participate, and factors which incline them to do that are likely to be associated with the factors causing their difficulties. Nevertheless, it is better to have a comparison group than not, so you should apply your measure(s) pre- and post-project to both groups. Don't try to make out your comparison group is a control group, though.

To get a true control group, you would list your 20 children, then allocate them randomly to 'control' or 'project' groups (by tossing a coin or using random number tables). Both groups would be pre-tested, then only the 'project' group invited to participate. However, not all of them might agree, so you would then have:

Control Group	Experimental Group
n = 10	Participating n = 5
	Not participating n = 5

In any event, the numbers quoted here in the experimental sub-groups are so small as to make comparisons of doubtful validity. A minimum sample size of ten is desirable to have any real confidence in your results.

So far we have talked about classical research design. But there are alternative approaches, which can be nearly as 'scientifically' acceptable and which can prove easier to do, especially where pre-existing data can be utilized. If for the students concerned there has been in the past a regular routine of applying attainment tests, historical data may be available for the project group. This enables you to scrutinize the fluctuations in progress in the past, and see how the gains during the project compare. This is called the (Interrupted) Time Series Design. Acceleration during the project should be fairly clearly evident in relation to previous rates of progress. Even better, and demanding little extra work, would be the inclusion of similar time series data from a comparison group.

As will already be evident, one of the problems with true control groups is that their use involves denying a service or facility to people who clearly seem to be in need of it. It can be argued that until you have demonstrated that the project has worked satisfactorily by using the control group, you don't actually know whether you are denying the control group anything worthwhile, but this logical contention does not tend to go down well with caring teachers.

A design which is useful in getting round this problem is the Discontinuity Design. Where a limited amount of a service or facility is available, there is often felt to be a moral obligation that all those in greatest need receive the service. If enough service is available to meet the needs of those who are worst off, but still leave some spare capacity, the limited surplus service may be extended to the larger band of those whose needs are less severe. But how to allocate the limited surplus to this large group? Arguably, random selection for project inclusion is the fairest way to go about it for this mid-band of students. Then the performance of otherwise similar included and non-included students around the margin of selection can be compared.

Finally, one further design is probably worth mentioning, which also gets round the ethical problems involving using control groups. This is the Multiple Baseline Design. If a larger group of potential clients exists than can be serviced at one time, they may have to be serviced by two consecutive projects. Where one half of the clients have to be serviced first, and the second later, it is reasonable and fair to allocate to 'early' and 'late' groups randomly. The gains of the 'early' group can be compared in the short run to the progress of the 'late' group. Subsequently, variations in procedure can be applied to one or other group, and gains compared within and between groups.

If you want to get really complicated, you could combine features of these designs. Other, more complex, designs are also possible. Whatever you choose to do, some attempt to guard against the Hawthorne Effect is necessary—the effect whereby the clients of an intervention show brief improvement purely because some attention is being paid to them and there is some element of novelty about the proceedings, quite irrespective of the actual nature of the intervention. Another possible source of embarrassment is the 'John Henry Effect'—where the control group, alerted to the fact that somebody considers them to be in need but is not providing anything for them, determines to improve anyway, and does so without apparent outside intervention.

Measures

The most frequently cited major objective for PAL projects is to raise attainment in some particular curriculum area. As it became clear that the Peer Assisted Learning process had a beneficial effect on the helpers also, as much attention came to be paid to measuring the gains of the helpers as to those of the helped. As project coordinators became aware of wider benefits, measures were increasingly applied to the attitudes, behavior and self-concept of both parties, both with reference to the PAL curriculum area and to other curriculum areas.

However, the project coordinator's time is limited, so decisions have to be made about how many and which evaluative measures are going to be applied to helper and helped respectively.

There are various basic requirements of any measures you seek to use. Economy of cost in materials and of time in administration and scoring are two obvious considerations. The measure needs to be reliable, in the sense of not being susceptible to wild, random fluctuations or erratic guesswork. It also needs to be valid, i.e. one must be assured that it actually measures what it is purporting to measure. Of equal importance, it needs to be relevant to the processes in question. Thus a phonic skills teaching program would probably not be relevantly evaluated by application of a reading test containing a very high proportion of irregular 'sight' words. Last, but by no means least, the measure must generate information which is analyzable. A vast quantity of impressionistic opinion may be fascinating to the project organizers, but will not enable them to communicate their findings to others in a clear and credible way.

Individual Versus Group Tests

The Peer Assisted Learning experience is nothing if not personal, involving as it does the development of a one-to-one relationship which persists over time and hopefully develops in quality, being characterized by rich and detailed feedback from helper to helped. During PAL, problems tend to be solved jointly as much as individually, and help is more or less always at hand. The relationship and the speed of progress through curriculum materials, which may themselves be completely individualized, is highly idiosyncratic.

To attempt to assess the impact of an experience of this kind by the use of some sort of group test, wherein the students sit in isolation in serried ranks and wrestle without help with some alien task, seems logically to be something of a nonsense—or is it?

If you wish to determine whether Peer Assisted Learning has improved the ability to function in a one-on-one situation, a measure administered to an individual personally would seem essential. But if you are anticipating that the PAL experience will produce results which will spread and endure outside of the PAL situation, then the application of a group test could be construed as a usefully stringent measure of generalization. However, remember that whatever the reliability of the group test quoted in the manual may be, with a small and idiosyncratically selected group of children with learning difficulties, reliability may be actually considerably less. Where group and individual tests have been used, correlation between the two kinds of test result might not be high. While the use of group tests may show substantial rates of gain taking the project group as a whole, individual results may seem so implausible that they should not be given much weight.

Peer monitoring can of course serve an assessment function as well as an intervention function. It could provide data enabling the evaluation of peer monitoring or other interventions, considering changes from baseline. Given this, it is important that the peer monitoring data is accurate and reliable. Much the same applies to peer assessment. These data can be cumulated over the course of a project and over all participants to give an indication of overall or summative impact.

Some PAL procedures incorporate peer-administered tests or probes which are integral to helping procedure, as in Cued Spelling, for example. This is a form of peer-administered curriculum based measurement. The teacher might use some form of regular and frequent curriculum based measurement—generalization tasks, probes, mini-tests delivered and scored by the teacher. These data can be similarly cumulated over the course of a project and over all participants as part of a summative evaluation.

Norm-referenced vs. Criterion-referenced

Norm-referenced tests allow a student's performance to be compared with that of many others in various parts of the country. Criterion referenced tests allow a student's performance to be compared with his or her own previous performance or some other benchmark of performance relevant to the curriculum. The first compares the student with other students, and the second compares the student's performance with a pre-determined criterion of skill acquisition. All tests have inherent problems. They may provoke anxiety in some students, making their individual results largely meaningless. For others, the unreality and apparent purposelessness of the exercise produces equally strange results. What the test means to the student might be quite different to what it means for the teacher.

In elderly norm-referenced tests, the content is often dated and of doubtful interest to some specific student sub-groups. The standardization data may be neither recent nor localized, and the data on supposed reliability and validity may be based on very small numbers. The structure of the test may itself be problematic, and you may find in some cases that answering only one or two more questions correctly produces a substantial shift in standardized score—the briefer the test, the more likely it is to suffer from this problem.

In some cases, there may be grave doubts about the cross-reliability of the supposedly 'parallel' forms of the test. Some evaluators have tried to get round this by allocating different parallel forms at random to students at pre-test, and the remaining forms at random at post-test. Another problem is that standardized tests were not designed for repeated use in short time spans on a pre-post basis to evaluate relatively short projects – there might be "practice effects" from familiarity with the format of the test even if the content is different in parallel forms.

In the reading area, standardized tests have included tasks of: word/ picture matching, individual word recognition, phonically regular word recognition, oral sentence reading, oral prose reading coupled with comprehension and recall questions, silent reading of signs, menus and directions coupled with comprehension questions, silent reading of continuous prose with cloze tasks, silent reading of sentences with multiple choice cloze tasks, and (would you believe!) having children read a real book and then answer questions on it.

By contrast, the advantage of criterion-referenced tests is that they can much more flexibly reflect the reality of the PAL curriculum. Their disadvantage is that comparison with national norms is no longer possible, and the absence of that vast, distant quasi-"control" group means that much more emphasis must be placed on achieving an adequate evaluation design. Basically, a criterion-referenced test checks whether the helped students have learned what they have been taught. While this may be simple and logical, such tests might not give information on how well the helped students can generalize new skills to other areas, unless this is built into the structure of the test. Nor may it be easy to obtain any idea of whether the student is accelerating at a rate that will eventually enable them to catch up with the average student.

In the reading area, Informal Reading Inventories (I.R.I.s) are a good example of this sort of device. An alternative possibility is some kind of cloze test based on curriculum material standard to the educational establishment, for instance basal readers or the core reading scheme. A word recognition test could be constructed from lists of high frequency words, or from designated social sight vocabulary.

Where a school is using a criterion-referenced measure of its own devising, it is worthwhile 'piloting' it with a relevant local sub-group first. A check on the stability of the measure with a normal sample in the school on a test-re-test, no-intervention basis would do, but would not necessarily reflect the stability of the measure with a sub-sample of 'abnormal' students. In any event, where standardized or criterion-referenced tests are in use, pre- and post-project measures should be carried out by the same person, to ensure that any bias (particularly to generosity in scoring) or other 'tester effects' hopefully will be the same on both occasions.

Instead of a straight attainment measure, some workers choose to evaluate by the deployment of a battery of 'diagnostic' tests. Some of these, such as 'miscue analysis' in the field of reading, can give useful information with practical implications for teaching and reflect qualitative changes in the learning style of students. However, other diagnostic tests are based on elaborate theoretical frameworks for which there is little sound empirical evidence, and may result in the drawing of no conclusions at all or the drawing of conclusions which have no practical import. Where sub-skills are to be measured as part of an evaluation with 'diagnostic' overtones, it is important that the real existence of those sub-skills and their practical relevance to the overall educational process is very clear.

Computer programs have become available to assist the teacher with the management of information about learning in the classroom. Forms of computerized curriculum based measurement can be both delivered to the student and scored by the computer, which then analyzes the results and advises the teacher of the outcome (and sometimes the diagnostic implications for action). They are sometimes termed "Learning Information Systems" (not to be confused with "Integrated Learning Systems", which also seek to incorporate individualized instruction and are much more expensive).

Another relatively recent development is the availability of norm-referenced tests of reading and mathematics which are delivered, scores and interpreted by the computer. Where such tests have a very large item bank, every test presented to every student on every occasion is different, which not only minimizes student cheating but also enables the tests to be taken very frequently without scores being inflated by practice effects as students get to learn the test content. Such tests are of course not as closely tied to the PAL curriculum as curriculum-based tests, but can still form a useful measure of student progress in terms of generalization of skills to novel content.

Educational Versus Social Gains

If social or emotional gains figure largely among your objectives for the project, you might wish to attempt some sort of measure of this, although to do so in such an area is fraught with difficulty, and doubts about reliability and validity will be great. Again, consideration is needed of whether these measures are to apply to helper, helped, or both.

A crude naturalistic indicator of improved behavior might be a reduced incidence of disciplinary referrals. There may be evidence of reductions in bullying, fighting and vandalism. Where data on these are not already collected through existing record systems, it may be worthwhile to have adults in regular contact with target children complete some form of rating, or a more specific checklist of problem behaviors, or more generalized observational assessments of problem behavior.

Direct observation with reference to some structured schedule is always valuable, but has the disadvantage of being very time consuming, so it is usually necessary to ask adults to make observations only in times when they would in any event be in contact with the relevant children. Of course, reductions in some of the more dramatic problem behaviors should not be routinely expected. In most cases, it will be interesting merely to see whether PAL partners interact with each other more outside of the PAL situation for the duration of the project, and at follow-up beyond. Naturalistic indicators such as choice of peers for teams and activity groups can be most revealing.

Beyond direct observation, there are a range of other measures, which may have the virtue of seeming quicker and easier, but which also raise more serious questions about relationship to everyday reality. Some form of sociometry is a particular favorite, on a before and after basis, to discern whether pairs develop any greater preference for each other on paper and pencil completion of peer preference lists. Attempts can be made to tap the more generalized attitudes of pairs to each other and the world in general, and this could be done verbally on an individual or group basis, or with no fewer threats to reliability via some form of simple questionnaire of controlled readability. Some project coordinators like to use paper and pencil 'tests' of self-concept or self-image, but some fairly erratic and implausible results have emerged from such exercises.

With all these measures, the issue of generalization needs to be addressed. Is it enough to have some form of evidence that social and emotional gains have occurred which are specific to the pair or the situation, or is it reasonable to expect these gains to generalize to ordinary classroom sessions, free-play times, or perhaps even to the community and home environments beyond the school boundary?

Behavioral Versus Attitudinal Data

Our discussion of the difficulties of evaluating social and emotional gains highlights a continuing quandary in research of this kind—the inconsistent relationship between what people feel and what they do.

In fact, of course, no single kind of data is wholly valid by itself, and it is useful to gather a mixture of kinds of data wherever possible, to obtain a fuller picture of what actually happened in a project from a variety of perspectives. This is known as "triangulation".

Behavioral measures can relate to either the process or outcome aspects of evaluation. They may include observation of required or desired behaviors during the project, in comparison with such behaviors occurring naturally during a baseline period or in comparison with those behaviors occurring spontaneously in a control group. Behavior cannot be observed continuously, and some form of subject-sampling, time-sampling or fixed-interval-sampling might be employed. In these cases, it is important to check on inter-observer reliability. It is of course possible to attempt to assess behavioral change in a much looser way by asking observers to complete rating scales, but these are much less reliable and suffer from a 'halo' effect. As we have already seen, there may be naturalistic indicators which are superficially behavioral but which certainly have affective and attitudinal overtones — like truancy and lateness rates.

Methodology for assessing 'attitudes' is problematic. The whole notion of 'attitudes' is highly nebulous. If you want people's feelings about the project, ask for them directly, but don't expect them necessarily to bear much relationship to the participants' actual behavior or even the gains shown in attainment. On the other hand, if you want people's observations of what participants actually did, ask for that directly, giving a 'no observations made' option. But do avoid confusing the two by asking for woolly generalized 'attitudes' or 'opinions'.

The views of the major participants in the project (helpers, helped, coordinators, and other professionals) should always be elicited. To rely simply on primitive instruments such as tests is to risk missing the texture of the reality of what happened. The participants will probably offer more process insights than summative conclusions, but the former must be actively elicited. Soliciting participant opinions serves not only to gather information, but also to clarify the information giver's mind on the subject, resolve any residual practical problems, and very often to recharge and commit the participants to continued effort.

A group meeting for all participants at the end of the project (or at the end of the initial 'push') is often a good idea. This could be audio- or video-recorded for more detailed analysis later (although an analysis of such complex data could prove a massive task). If time is available, individual interviews with at least a sample of the helpers according to some semi-structured format is desirable. Similar interviews with the helped students and professionals are desirable, but should preferably be carried out by an 'outsider' to the project if they are to be objective.

Realistically, time constraints and/or the need to have readily analyzable data often drive people into using some form of questionnaire. However, there are very large doubts about the reliability and validity of responses to paper-and-pencil measures. In the construction of questionnaires, the project leaders must decide which questions are important to them, but the device must be structured to eliminate any possibility of leading respondents into giving a particular answer. A multiple-choice format gives easily analyzable data, but is crude and simplistic, while an open-ended format is dependent on the free-writing skills of the respondents and yields data which is often difficult to analyze. A balance between the two is usual. Some overall index of consumer satisfaction is desirable, and a useful acid test is always the question: 'Would you recommend the project to a friend?'

Lying somewhere in the middle ground between behavioral and attitudinal measures are various techniques of 'self-recording'. Participants may keep simple written records on themselves and/or each other in the form of points, grades, ratings, or general comments or quantitative notes of task completed, time taken, etc. In some projects, participants make audio or video recordings of themselves for later viewing and/or rating by themselves and/or others. This kind of self-evaluation is often valuable for keeping participants on-task.

Generalization and Maintenance

Are the gains made in the Peer Assisted Learning situation specific to that situation, or do we expect them to generalize—to other situations, to other (non-targeted) skills or problems, to other resource materials, or to other helping or helped students? If we do expect this, how are we to measure it? Most difficult of all, how are we to measure it easily?

The other thorny question is that of long-term duration of gains made. Many teaching programs have shown reasonable results in the short-term, but the gains produced have often 'washed out' in comparison to control groups at two year follow-up. So some form of follow-up evaluation is important, preferably together with follow-up of a control or comparison group. Such an exercise is often made difficult by the loss of subjects from one or both groups—'sample attrition'.

On the other hand, it is also reasonable to ask how long you can sensibly expect a relatively brief and lightweight' intervention to continue to demonstrate an impact on the highly complex and cumulative learning process.

Where Time Series evaluative data on attainment is routinely collected on a yearly basis in school, follow-up evaluation research is greatly facilitated.

Analysis of Data

There is a great difference between statistical and educational significance. Where a very large sample is used, statistical significance is much easier to achieve. Where a very large number of different outcome measures are used, the chances are that one or two will show statistically significant changes irrespective of any real impact of the project. If a project with large samples produces gains which are only just statistically significant, searching questions need to be asked about the educational significance of the results. Was it worth all that time and effort for such a small skill increment?

For those unsure of their competence in statistical analysis, or doubting the validity of the procedures, simple comparison of raw data on scattergrams or graphing of shifts in averages for groups gives a ready visual indication of changes. Certainly the data is worth summarizing in this sort of way for feedback to the participants, who may be assumed to be statistically unsophisticated.

Evaluation Results Feedback and Dissemination

One of the disadvantages of complex data analysis is that it takes time, and very often early feedback of evaluation results to the project participants is highly desirable, to renew their commitment and recharge their energies. A simple graph and/or brief table of average scores for the group is probably the best vehicle for this—remember, the results must be understood by the learners as well.

The unreliability of standardized tests makes giving individual test scores to the participants a risky business, and care must be taken throughout not to give undue emphasis to test data as distinct from other types. Any individual scores are probably best given in an individual interview rather than a group meeting situation, if at all.

In any event, it is probably best for one person to take responsibility for collating and presenting the evaluation data, or it might lie about on scraps of paper forever. Evaluation results have a number of other uses. Publicity via the local press, professional journals, curriculum bulletins or in-service meetings not only helps to disseminate good practice and help more children, it also serves to boost the morale of the project initiators and participants. The results may be useful to convince skeptics on the school staff, generate a wider interest and produce a more coherent future policy on Peer Assisted Learning in the school.

The school governors will be interested, as should be various officers of the State or School District education authority. A demonstration of cost-effectiveness may elicit more tangible support from administration or elected representatives. Associated services such as library services, advisory services, resource materials centers and so on might be drawn into the network of community support by a convincing evaluation report.

And so to the final word. If you get results you don't like, you'll spend hours puzzling over them trying to explain them away. Make sure that if you get results you do like, you spend as much time and energy searching for other factors outside the project that could have produced them. If you don't spot them, someone else might—and probably will!

9

Embedding and Extending PAL

Education suffers greatly from short-lived initiatives which enjoy a brief period of being fashionable, then fall out of favor and disappear without trace. It is worrying that some of these initiatives seem to become fashionable even though there is no good evidence for their effectiveness. It is even more worrying that some seem to go out of fashion even when there *is* good evidence that they are effective.

Peer Assisted Learning has been around for a few thousand years, but in schools it has been subject to cycles of higher and lower usage over the last two hundred years. These cycles have largely been the product of political and economic factors related to the sociology of the teaching profession.

Fortunately, Peer Assisted Learning currently enjoys a resurgence and expansion of growth in usage, and qualitative development and extension to new varieties of PAL. However, history warns us that this might not automatically continue forever.

We hope that by following the guidelines in this book, you will have enjoyed success for yourself, the helpers and the helped. Now it is time to think about consolidation—embedding Peer Assisted Learning within the school organization so that it continues to maximize student potential, enduring through whatever political, financial, sociological or other tides that might flow your way.

In addition to embedding PAL as part of continuing mainstream practice, you will wish to consider extending it:

- to more helpers and helped
- to helpers and helped with greater difficulties
- to other subject areas
- to other classes and colleagues
- to other PAL methods
- to all channels in the PAL model

The potential is enormous. But as ever, remember that a modest development done well is better than a large development done badly.

Developing a Whole School Approach

There is no better apprenticeship for being a helper than being helped. Many schools with cross-year class wide PAL programs actively promote the equal opportunity and apprenticeship advantages of this model—every student who is helped in a lower grade fully expects from the outset to become a tutor when in a higher grade. As students are helped in preparation for becoming helpers, any ambivalence about receiving help decreases and motivation to learn often increases. The asymmetry between helper and helped is reduced, and the stigma often otherwise associated with receiving help disappears. All the students have the chance to participate and the opportunity to help, which makes them all feel equally valuable and worthwhile.

Sometimes students who are helped in one subject are simultaneously helpers to students in a lower grade in the same subject. Those who are helped in one subject might be helpers to their own age peers in another subject. Even the most able student in any grade can be presented with problems that require the help of an even more capable student from a higher grade, and thereby learn that no-one is as smart as all of us. The symbiosis of the helper and helped roles is something upon which to consciously capitalize.

Over time a critical mass of teachers who support PAL can develop in the school, although a few remaining colleagues might always have difficulty adapting to the role of manager of flexible and effective learning rather than that of direct transmitter of traditional wisdom. PAL builds on students' strengths and mobilizes them as active participants in the learning process. Not only do helpers learn the subject better and deeper, but they also learn transferable skills in helping and cooperation, listening and communication. All of this influences the school ethos, developing a cultural norm of helping and caring. PAL contributes to a sense of cohesive community and encourages personal and social development. Eventually, Peer Assisted Learning can permeate the whole ethos of a school and be deployed spontaneously in many areas of the curriculum.

Although every working day they are part of a very busy community, teachers all too often feel strangely isolated. Finding time together to have a discussion about anything is difficult enough—and at the end of the school day, energies are at a low ebb for professional discussions. Ideally, time should be scheduled to bring teachers together regularly in mutual support and problem-solving gatherings where they can share their ideas, materials and methods—and build each other's confidence and self-esteem. Peer Assisted Learning works very well with teachers, too!

Another problem arises from changes of professional personnel. Frequently the kind of teacher who is first to innovate within a school is also the kind that is offered promotion soonest, which might take them to another district or school—a gain for the receiving school, but a serious loss for the previous school. Arranging for skills to be passed on before innovators depart is essential to manage human resources effectively.

These difficulties hinder attempts to develop all coordinated whole school developments, of course, not only Peer Assisted Learning. While forward planning and energy are needed to overcome them, the rewards are great.

An Experimental Evaluation

A two-semester program was developed by the Peer Research Laboratory and implemented in six low socio-economic status New York City public high schools with records of high student dropout rates (Gartner and Riessman, 1995).

Three program features were introduced in three randomly assigned experimental schools:

- Tutees were involved in activities to promote joint program ownership, such as group meetings with tutors for planning, training, program assessment and sharing of their experiences. These meetings were facilitated by an adult teacher-coordinator at each site.
- Tutees were given an opportunity to become tutors the following semester, if they passed the course in which they were being tutored (with a grade of 75 or higher) and they were absent from the group meetings no more than two times.
- Tutees were provided with a stipend for participation in the group meetings, but not for receiving tutoring.

In three matched control schools, tutees received a traditional tutorial program without these features. To balance the weekly group meetings in the experimental schools, control school tutees met once a week with the teacher-coordinator to discuss their progress and needs.

Compared to the control group receiving regular tutoring, the experimental students showed: higher program attendance (91 percent compared to 70 percent); significantly higher grades in the first semester in tutored subjects (78.3 compared to 65.4); higher rates of completion in tutored courses (14 percent of students in the fall semester and seven percent of students in the spring semester had not completed their courses compared to 22 percent in the fall and 13 percent in the spring for students in control schools).

Ensuring Sustained Success

So "cascaded" Peer Assisted Learning clearly adds extra value. But how are we to *ensure* the longer term success of PAL strategies? Embedding PAL within an organization or larger community requires careful attention to the needs of the learners, the professional educators, and the wider system. In order for a PAL initiative to last and grow, there are some considerations that should be met. If you want your Peer Assisted Learning initiative to (a) last and/or (b) spread, consider the following:

Cost-Benefit Balance for All

The benefits must outweigh the costs *for all concerned* if the initiative is to endure. For the initiating teacher, costs will be in terms of time devoted, materials and other resources, and the general harassment and stress involved in doing anything new. All of these must be kept as low as possible. On the benefit side, the teacher will need both subjective and objective evidence of impact in relation to the objectives set.

More than that, the initiative also has to *feel good*—have a warm and satisfying social and emotional tone—this will benefit from a little deliberate cultivation. However, no teacher is an island, and the initiative also needs to be compatible with the current local philosophy, political correctness and mood of the professional peer group and senior policy dictators. Fortunately, Peer Assisted Learning has largely escaped adverse politicization—it is right up there with motherhood and apple pie in terms of acceptability.

A similar analysis can be applied to the other participants—the helpers, the helped students, and the head of the institution. They also need minimization of time wastage and harassment, need to feel good about the project, need to be clear what they are getting out of it and what the other participants are getting out of it, and need to be able to confidently assert their support for it in the face of incredulity from their peer group.

Objectives and Applications

Be clear about the different objectives for different types of Peer Assisted Learning. Your objectives for a specific project might be in the cognitive, affective or social domain, or some combination. Don't let someone else evaluate your project against a different set of objectives!

Choose your format to suit your context, objectives and possibilities. Consider which formats will suit which subjects, topics, activities, classes, rooms, and so on. Use a mixture of cross age and same age, cross ability and same ability, fixed role and reciprocal role methods as necessary and optimal.

Plan for flexibility. If you work at it you can figure out a format or method which will fit into almost any local exigencies: complex organizations, highly structured timetables, lack of physical space, lack of appropriate furniture, poor acoustics, rigid attitudes in adults in positions of power, rigid attitudes in children who have learned to prefer passive inertia, and so on. But don't be too ambitious to start with—many small steps get you there quickest in the end.

Materials, Methods and Monitoring

Materials should preferably be low cost, already to hand, differentiated for different needs, attractive and durable. A simple system for access to and exchange of the necessary materials is needed. Tracking current possession of items might be necessary, but don't get hung up with bureaucracy that makes work.

Prescribe a clear and simple method for interaction to start with. Ensure the participants always receive good quality training. Remember methods need to be truly and consistently interactive, or one partner will go to sleep. Ensure the method involves modeling as well as much discussion, questioning and explaining. Ensure there are clear procedures for the identification, diagnosis and correction of errors.

Ensure the method builds in and capitalizes on intrinsic satisfaction for all participants. Once the participants are experiencing success, ensure they do not become dependent on a routine method, and make clear the times and opportunities within which they are encouraged and even required to be creative and take the initiative.

Close monitoring of participant behavior is especially necessary at the beginning, where student deviation can lead to failure which will be attributed to you. After an initial period of "getting it right", creative and reflective deviance in students might be encouraged, but will need close monitoring. In the longer run, some "drift" is almost inevitable—keep checking to see that it is productive.

Rejuvenation, Evaluation and Iteration

Initiating a project (especially in an inert environment) is very demanding in terms of time and energy, although that capital investment is almost always considered worthwhile later. Once things are up and running smoothly, it is tempting to either relax, or rush on and start another project with a different group. The latter is more dangerous than the former—don't spread yourself too thinly. After a few weeks or months most initiatives need some rejuvenation—not necessarily an organizational improvement, just a change to inject some novelty.

Fortunately, Peer Assisted Learning is very flexible and offers many ways for injecting variety and novelty—change of partners, subject topics or activities, format of operation, and so on. However, please do not try to use it for everything, or you will overdose the learners. It can enhance productivity to give them a rest and then return to a modified format not too long afterwards. In any event. Close consultation with the students always adds extra momentum to their motivation—even if their suggestions are contradictory and cannot all be implemented, the feeling that their views are valued increases commitment to the onward process.

Projects must target gains for all participants (particularly the helpers). Evaluation should also seek to check whether there are longer term as well as short term gains, and whether helping generalizes outside the specifically nominated PAL sessions.

You might wish to consider to what extent you can give away some of the organization and management to the children themselves. Obviously you would need to check on this from time to time, especially with younger children. Of course, you would wish positives to be accentuated and negatives to be eliminated. Keeping the feel good factor going is important. However, a degree of self management (which can include self monitoring) can heighten self-esteem and responsibility and help to make initiatives self sustaining.

Once Peer Assisted Learning is accepted and deployed by more staff, some co-ordination will be necessary. Working together, you can build iterative cycles of involvement in different kinds of Peer Assisted Learning in different formats with all children in role as helpers and as helped at different times, in a developmental progressive sequence.

Beyond this, however, are the systemic implications of frequent, various and equal opportunities for all to be both helper and helped. These lead to a positive ethos in which Peer Assisted Learning is accepted as something "normal" permeating everyday life—a learning tool as natural as opening a book or turning on a computer. When you see your students explaining to a newcomer from another district what Peer Assisted Learning is all about, and showing amazement on discovering that everybody doesn't do it everywhere, you will know you have got it embedded.

PAL Beyond School

Cross-school Peer Assisted Learning is difficult to schedule, particularly between elementary and high schools. However, the quality of interaction can be worth the extra trouble, especially for some of the less able helpers. Many universities and colleges now have programs to enable their own students to visit both elementary and high schools to act as "peer" helpers—although the age gap can be considerable, the role modeling and impact on raising the aspirations of the helped students adds extra value. Peer Assisted Learning of various types is also increasingly common within colleges and universities, so PAL at elementary school forms an apprenticeship for PAL at high school and for PAL at college.

Beyond educational institutions, Peer Assisted Learning can also be found in informal community education and both formally and informally in the workplace. The transferable PAL skills developed by students in elementary school can continue to be effectively applied for the next 50 years. Some of these skills also have high transfer into parenting skills. Peer Assisted Learning treats learners as catalysts in their own growth and development, as well as contributors to the lives of others. PAL stimulates, supports and sustains lifelong learning. It is truly fit for the future.

10

Sources and Resources

General

The National Peer Helpers Association, P.O. Box 2684, Greenville, NC 27858, USA publishes the Peer Facilitator Quarterly, which includes many articles on peer education and addresses issues of evaluation as well as practice. Also available is a very substantial bibliography on various aspects of peer education and helping. An annual NPHA conference is held in the USA. www.peerhelping.org/

The National Tutoring Association (www.NTATutor.org) also offers annual conferences and a regular newsletter.

Peer Resources, 1052 Davie Street, Victoria, British Columbia V8S 4E3, Canada produce a catalogue including many practical resources for various types of peer assisted learning, counseling and helping. They also operate training institutes and provide bibliographies. (www.peer.ca/peer.html and email rcarr@islandnet.com).

Mentoring and Tutoring is a practitioners' journal produced by Carfax (www.carfax.co.uk)

Further General Reading

Aldrich, S. & Wright, J. (undated) *Peer Tutoring: A Multimedia Manual.* (www.scsd.k12.ny.us/sbit/dirhtml/libfile/libdocs/software/ peertut.pdf).
A public domain practical manual with some reproducible materials developed in the Syracuse City School District, New York State.

Allen, V. L., Ed. (1976) *Children as Teachers: Theory and Research on Tutoring.* New York: Academic Press.
A timeless classic.

Bloom, S., Ed. (1975) *Peer and Cross-Age Tutoring in the Schools: An Individualized Supplement to Group Instruction.* Washington, DC: US Department of Health, Education and Welfare (ERIC ED 118543).
Governments keep re-discovering this topic around the world.

Ehly, S. W. and Larsen, S.C. (1980) *Peer Tutoring for Individualized Instruction.* Boston: Allyn and Bacon.
Much sensible advice, still relevant.

Gartner, A., Kohler, M. and Riessman, F. (1971) *Children Teach Children: Learning by Teaching.* New York: Harper and Row.
Another classic.

O'Donnell, A. M. & King, A., Ed. (1999) *Cognitive Perspectives on Peer Learning.* Mahwah, NJ & London: Lawrence Erlbaum.
Much more academic than practical, but up-to-date. (www.erlbaum.com).

Topping, K. J. & Ehly, S., Ed. (1998) *Peer Assisted Learning.* Mahwah NJ & London: Lawrence Erlbaum.
Gives much more detail and research evidence about the approaches outlined in this Practical Guide, as well as Peer Education and Peer Counseling, with an extended Resources listing. (www.erlbaum.com).

Paired Learning

Topping, K. J. (1995). *Paired Reading, Spelling and Writing: The Handbook for Teachers and Parents*. London & New York: Cassell. www.cassell.co.uk

Topping, K. J. (2001) *Thinking, Reading, Writing: A Practical Guide To Paired Learning with Peers, Parents & Volunteers*. New York & London: Continuum International.

Read On Web Site (www.dundee.ac.uk/psychology/ReadOn).
For the extension of Paired (Duolog) Reading into higher order reading and thinking skills. Gives details of the Read On video pack (PAL video format only).

Topping, K. J. (1997). *Duolog Reading: A Video Training Pack* (video). Madison, WI: Institute for Academic Excellence (NTSC video format only). www.advlearn.com

Paired Reading: Positive Reading Practice (video).
The Teacher's Manual and NTSC format training video are available from the North Alberta Reading Specialists' Council, Box 9538, Edmonton, Alberta T6E 5X2, Canada.

Topping, K. J. & Bamford, J. (1998). *Parental Involvement and Peer Tutoring in Mathematics and Science: Developing Paired Maths into Paired Science*. London: Fulton; Bristol, PA: Taylor & Francis. www.fultonbooks.co.uk

Topping, K. J. & Bamford, J. (1998). *The Paired Maths Handbook: Parental Involvement and Peer Tutoring in Mathematics*. London: Fulton; Bristol, PA : Taylor & Francis. www.fultonbooks.co.uk

Topping, K. J. (1998). *The Paired Science Handbook: Parental Involvement and Peer Tutoring in Science*. London: Fulton; Bristol, PA: Taylor & Francis. www.fultonbooks.co.uk
An updated bibliography will be found on the author's web site at www.dundee.ac.uk/psychology/kjtopping.

Pause Prompt Praise

Merrett, F. (1994). *Improving Reading: A Teacher's Guide to Peer Tutoring.* London: David Fulton. www.fultonbooks.co.uk
Despite the general title, mostly about Pause Prompt Praise.

Juniper Gardens. *Class Wide Peer Tutoring.* Juniper Gardens Children's Project, 650 Minnesota Avenue, Second Floor, Kansas City, KS 66101. www.lsi.ukans.edu/jg/jgcpindx.htm

Greenwood, C. R., Delquadri, J., & Carta, J. J. (1988). *Class Wide Peer Tutoring (CWPT): Teachers manual.*
Available form Juniper Gardens Children's Project.

Greenwood, C. R., Terry, B. J., Delquadri, J., Elliott, M., & Arreaga-Mayer, C. (1995). *Class Wide Peer Tutoring (CWPT): Effective teaching and research review.*
Available form Juniper Gardens Children's Project.

The PALS Program in Reading & Math

Doug & Lynn Fuchs at Vanderbilt University
www.vanderbilt.edu/CASL/reports.html

Fuchs, D., & Fuchs, L.S. (1998). Researchers and teachers working closely together to adapt instruction for diverse learners. *Learning Disability Research and Practice, 13*, 126-137.
Summarizes the research program on reading PALS, along with the research-to-practice model, by which researchers and teachers collaboratively developed and tested PALS.

Fuchs, L.S., Fuchs, D., Kazdan, S., & Allen, S. (1999). Effects of peer-assisted learning strategies in reading with and without training in elaborated help giving. *Elementary School Journal, 99*, 201-220.
Reports a study that examined the contribution of student training in elaborated help giving within reading PALS; results showed that

(a) at the intermediate grades, elaborated help giving, in which students helped partners figure out unknown words and main ideas on their own, enhanced reading achievement, but (b) at the primary grades, students achieved better with the standard PALS, without the additional of elaborated help-giving strategies.)

Mathes, P.G., Howard, J.K., Allen, S.H., & Fuchs, D. (1998). Peer-assisted learning strategies for first-grade readers: Responding to the needs of diverse learners. *Reading Research Quarterly, 33*, 62-94.
Reports a study examining the effectiveness of reading PALS at the first-grade level; findings support the efficacy of PALS for low- and average-performing first graders and document that PALS does not harm high-achieving first graders.

Fuchs, LS., Fuchs, D., Hamlett, C.L., Phillips, N.B., Karns, K., & Dutka, S. (1997). Enhancing students' helping behaviour during peer-mediated instruction with conceptual mathematical explanations. *Elementary School Journal, 97*, 223-250.
Presents a study examining the added-value of preparing students' to formulate conceptual mathematical explanations during PALS; results showed that (a) students with LD, as well as other low-, average-, and high-performing classmates, provided better explanations more when taught to formulate conceptual explanations, and (b) students who were taught methods to formulate conceptual mathematical explanations achieved better in mathematics. Based on the study, PALS incorporates training for students in formulating conceptual mathematical explanations.)

Phillips, N.B., Hamlett, C.L., Fuchs, L.S., & Fuchs, D. (1993). Combining classwide curriculum-based measurement and peer tutoring to help general educators provide adaptive education. *Learning Disabilities Research and Practice, 8*, 148-156.
Provides an overview of the math PALS methods for practitioners, with a brief summary of an efficacy study.

Peer Tutoring in General

It is always worth searching the larger on-line bookstores for new titles in peer-assisted learning.

Foster, E. (1992). *Tutoring, Learning by Helping: Student handbook for training peer and cross-age tutors.* Educational Media Corporation.

Jenkins, J. R., & Jenkins, L. M. (1981). *Cross-age and peer tutoring: Help for students with learning problems.* Reston, VA: Council for Exceptional Children.

Maxwell, M. (1994). *When Tutor Meets Student.* University of Michigan Press.

Peer Modelling

Schunk, D. H. (1987). Peer models and children's behavioral change. *Review of Educational Research, 57,* 149-174.

Schunk, D. H. (1996). *Learning Theories: An educational perspective.* (2nd ed.). Englewood Cliffs, NJ: Men-ill. (See chap. 4).

Schunk, D. H., & Hanson, A. R. (1985). Peer models: Influence on children's self-efficacy and achievement. *Journal of Educational Psychology, 77,* 313-322.

Schunk, D. H., Hanson, A. R., & Cox, P. D. (1987). Peer model attributes and children's achievement behaviors. *Journal of Educational Psychology, 79,* 54-61.

Peer Monitoring

Brown, C. C., Topping, K. J., Henington, C. & Skinner, C. H. (1999). Peer monitoring of learning behavior: The case of "Checking Chums". *Educational Psychology in Practice, 15 (3),* 174-182

Kalfus, G. R. (1984). Peer mediated intervention: A critical review. *Child and Family Behavior Therapy, 6,* 17–43.

Saudargas, R. A., & Fellers, G. (1986). *State-event Classroom Observation System.* (Research edition). Knoxville, TN: University of Tennessee, Department of Psychology. (Dr. Richard Saudargas, Psychology Department, University of Tennessee, Knoxville, TN 37996).

Shapiro, E. S. (1996). *Academic Skills Problems: Direct Assessment and Intervention* (2nd ed.). New York: Guilford.

School Psychology Review, 21, (1992).
Special interest miniseries on self-management interventions in the schools.

Peer Assessment

Bratcher, S. (1994). *Evaluating Children's Writing.* NY: St. Martin's Press.

Carlson, D.M. & Roellich, C. (1983, April 14-16). *Teaching Writing Easily and Effectively to Get Results: The Evaluation Process.* Paper presented at the Annual Meeting of the National Council of Teachers of English, Seattle WA.
A guide for teachers in developing student skills in analysis, evaluation, proof-reading. Rating scale for grades 6-12 included. Available from ERIC.

Christensen, L, Haugen, N.S. and Kean, J.M. (1982). A Guide to Teaching Self/Peer Editing. [Booklet]. Madison, WI: School of Education, University of Wisconsin-Madison.
Procedures/techniques for teachers at elementary, middle & high school levels. Appendices with resources.) Available from ERIC.

Peer Counseling & Education

Information about Judith Tindall's Accelerated Development titles will be found at www.taylorandfrancis.com/ad/peer99cat.htm. Many more peer counseling and peer education resources are listed in Topping and Ehly (see above).

Peer Assisted Learning: A Brief Guide

What is Peer Assisted Learning?

Part of life at school asks children to try to do better than other children. But another very important part of school and later life is working with and helping other people. Children learn well in both ways.

Peer Assisted Learning (PAL) means having children help other children to learn. Sometimes older children help younger children, and sometimes more able children help less able children of the same age.

It is important that Peer Assisted Learning is set up in a way that makes sure that the student who is helping gets something out of it, as well as the student who is helped.

Peer Assisted Learning is used for only a small part of the school day. It increases the effectiveness of regular teaching directly by the class teacher, which still forms by far the biggest part of schooling.

History

The idea is a very old one, first noted about 400 years ago. In Britain, Bell and Lancaster used peer tutoring a lot about 200 years ago. By 1816, 100,000 children were learning in this way. Peer tutoring then caught on in quite a few parts of the world.

From 1960 onwards, peer tutoring was used more and more, especially in the United States. Other ways for children to help other children were tried out. "Peer Assisted Learning" is the general name covering all the different kinds of peer tutoring and these newer ways of helping.

Teachers in many different kinds of schools have found that Peer Assisted Learning is a great 'boost' for all children. Today, Peer Assisted Learning is spreading rapidly in many parts of the world.

Effects

Many Peer Assisted Learning projects work on reading, the most important skill of all. But Peer Assisted Learning has also been used with a very wide range of other subjects, including mathematics, spelling, writing, languages, science, thinking skills and computer skills.

The helpers gain as much as, if not more than, the students who are helped. So helpers are not just being 'used'. To be able to help in a subject, you have to really get to understand it well and be able to explain it. So helping helps the helpers learn faster, too.

There is no doubt that Peer Assisted Learning 'works'. There is a lot of research over many years proving that in Peer Assisted Learning projects, the helpers improve in the subject area as much, if not more than, the students who are helped, but at their own level. Many studies show that Peer Assisted Learning also improves how both helper and helped feel about the subject area—they get to like it more. Also, in many cases the helper and helped grow to like each other more, and get on better. There are also many reports of both helper and helped showing more confidence and better behavior. The research clearly shows that peer helping is a highly effective way of using school time.

Some projects have helpers and helped students of the same age, and some have older children as the helpers. Any difference in age does not seem to matter, as long as the helper is more able in the subject area than the helped. If the helpers and helped are not too far apart in age and ability, there is more chance of the helper improving in the subject as a result. Some schools are now also organizing Peer Assisted Learning with pairs of the same ability, where the job of helper switches from one to the other (this needs very careful planning).

Planning

Peer Assisted Learning takes time and care to set up properly, and it is the professional teacher who has the skill to do this. Careful plans must be made for matching students, finding the right sort of materials, training helping and helped students, and many other points of organization. However, this time is worthwhile, to ensure the Peer Assisted Learning is very effective. Teachers often start Peer Assisted Learning in reading, but then become more confident in using the method in other subject areas. Like any other way of effective teaching or managing learning, setting up peer helper projects needs enthusiasm, careful planning and hard work on the part of the teacher. Peer Assisted Learning is not an easy option.

Scope

Some elementary schools are now offering all young children the chance to be helped by a peer, and all the older children the chance to be a helper. This serves to settle the young children into the school socially, and gives a boost to the older children, who feel very grown-up and responsible. In high schools parents can often lose touch with what their children are doing, but Peer Assisted Learning is often more and more popular with children as they move up through the school. For many pairs, Peer Assisted Learning has good spin-off in terms of better social harmony and more interest in other subject areas.

Further Reading

Topping, K. J. (2000) *Peer Assisted Learning: A Practical Guide for Teachers.* Cambridge, MA: Brookline Books.

References

Allen, V. L. (Ed.) (1976) *Children as teachers: theory and research on tutoring*. New York: Academic Press.

Arreaga-Mayer, C., Terry, B. and Greenwood, C. (1998) Classwide peer tutoring. In K. J. Topping and S. Ehly (Eds.) *Peer-assisted learning*. Mahwah NJ and London UK: Lawrence Erlbaum Associates.

Bell, A. (1797). *An experiment in education made at the male asylum of Madras: suggesting a system by which a school or family may teach itself under the superintendence of the master or parent*. London: Cadell & Davis.

Bloom, B. S. (1984). The search for methods of group instruction as effective as one-to-one tutoring. *Educational Leadership, 41* (8), 4-17.

Bloom, S. (Ed.) (1975). *Peer and cross-age tutoring in the schools*. Washington, DC: US Department of Health, Education and Welfare. (ERIC Document ED 118543)

Brown, C. C., Topping, K. J., Henington, C. and Skinner, C. H. (1999) Peer monitoring of learning behaviour: the case of "Checking Chums". *Educational Psychology in Practice, 15* (3), 174-182.

Cameron, J. and Pierce, D. (1994) Reinforcement, reward and intrinsic motivation: a meta-analysis. *Review of Educational Research, 64 (3)*, 363-423.

Charconnet, M. (1975). Peer tutoring: operational description of various systems and their applications. In *Development of educational methods and techniques adapted to the specific conditions of the developing countries*. Paris: UNESCO.

Cohen, P. A., Kulik, J. A. and Kulik, C-L. C. (1982). Educational outcomes of tutoring: a meta-analysis of findings. *American Educational Research Journal, 19 (2)*, 237-48.

Custer, J. D. and Osguthorpe, R. T. (1983). Improving social acceptance by training handicapped students to tutor their nonhandicapped peers. *Exceptional Children, 50 (2),* 173-5.

Devin-Sheehan, L., et al. (1976). Research on children tutoring children: a critical review. *Review of Educational Research, 46 (3),* 355-85.

Dweck, C. S. and Bush, E. S. (1976). Sex differences in learned helplessness: differential debilitation with peer and adult evaluators. *Developmental Psychology, 12 (2),* 1.

Eberwein, L., et al. (1976). *An annotated bibliography on volunteer tutoring programs.* Paper presented at the south-east region reading conference of the International Reading Association. (ERIC Document ED 117662)

Fantuzzo, J. and Ginsburg-Block, M. (1998). Reciprocal peer tutoring: developing and testing effective peer collaborations for elementary school students. In K. J. Topping and S. Ehly (Eds.) *Peer-assisted learning.* Mahwah NJ and London UK: Lawrence Erlbaum Associates.

Feldman, R. S., Devin-Sheehan, L. and Allen, V. L. (1976). Children tutoring children: a critical review of research. In V. L. Allen (Ed.) *Children as teachers: Theory and research on tutoring.* New York: Academic Press.

Fitz-Gibbon, C. T. and Reay, D. G. (1982). Peer tutoring: Brightening up F. L. teaching in an urban comprehensive school. *British Journal of Language Teaching, 20 (1),* 39-44.

Gartner, S., Kohler, M. and Riessman, F. (1971). *Children teach children: Learning by teaching.* New York: Harper & Row.

Gartner, A. and Riessman, F. (1995). *A new peer tutoring design.* New York: Peer Research Laboratory.

Gerber, M. and Kauffman, J. M. (1981). Peer tutoring in academic settings. In P. S. Strain (Ed.) *The utilization of classroom peers as behavior change agents.* New York and London: Plenum Press.

Glynn, T. (1996). Pause Prompt Praise: Reading tutoring procedures for home and school partnership. In S. W. Wolfendale & K. J. Topping (Eds.) *Family involvement in literacy: Effective partnerships in education.* London and New York: Cassell.

Goldstein, H. and Wickstrom, S. (1986). Peer intervention effects on communicative interaction among handicapped and nonhandicapped preschoolers. *Journal of Applied Behavior Analysis, 19 (2),* 209-14.

Goodlad, S. (1979). *Learning by teaching: An introduction to tutoring.* London: Community Service Volunteers.

Greenwood, C. R., Carta, J. J. and Kamps, D. (1990). Teacher-mediated versus peer-mediated instruction: A review of educational advantages and disadvantages. In H. C. Foot, M. J. Morgan and R. H. Shute (Eds.), *Children helping children.* London & New York: John Wiley.

Henington, C. and Skinner, C. H. (1998). Peer monitoring. In K. J. Topping and S. Ehly (Eds.) *Peer-assisted learning.* Mahwah NJ and London UK: Lawrence Erlbaum Associates.

Henry, S. E. (1979). Sex and locus of control as determinants of children's responses to peer versus adult praise. *Journal of Educational Psychology, 71 (5),* 605.

Johnson, R. T. and Johnson, D. W. (1983). Effects of co-operative, competitive and individualistic learning experiences on social development. *Exceptional Children, 49 (4),* 323-329.

Klaus, D. J. (1975). *Patterns of peer tutoring.* Washington, DC: American Institutes of Research. (ERIC Document ED 103356)

Lancaster, J. (1803). *Improvements in education as it respects the industrious classes of the community, containing, among other important particulars, an account of the institution for the education of one thousand poor children, Borough Road, Southwark; and of the new system of education on which it is conducted.* London: Darton & Harvey.

Levine, H. M., Glass, G. V. and Meister, G. R. (1987). A cost-effectiveness analysis of computer-assisted instruction. *Evaluation Review, 11 (1)*, 50-72.

McCurdy, B. L. and Shapiro, E. S. (1992). A comparison of teacher-monitoring, peer-monitoring, and self-monitoring with curriculum-based measurement in reading among students with learning disabilities. *Journal of Special Education, 26 (2)*, 162-180.

Maheady, L. (1998). Advantages and disadvantages of peer-assisted learning strategies. In K. J. Topping and S. Ehly (Eds.) *Peer-assisted learning*. Mahwah NJ and London UK: Lawrence Erlbaum Associates.

Maheady, L. and Harper, G. F. (1987). A classwide peer tutoring program to improve the spelling test performance of low income, third- and fourth-grade students. *Education and Treatment of Children, 10*, 120-133.

Maheady, L., Sacca, M. K. and Harper, G. F. (1988). Classwide peer tutoring with mildly handicapped high school students. *Exceptional Children, 55*, 52-59.

Maher, C. A. (1982). Behavioral effects of using conduct problem adolescents as cross-age tutors. *Psychology in the Schools, 19*, 360-64.

Maher, C. A., Maher, B. C., and Thurston, C. J. (1998). Disruptive students as tutors: A systems approach to planning and evaluation of programs. In K. J. Topping and S. Ehly (Eds.) *Peer-assisted learning*. Mahwah NJ and London UK: Lawrence Erlbaum Associates.

Mathes, P. G., Howard, J. K., Allen, S. H. and Fuchs, D. (1998). Peer-assisted learning strategies for first-grade readers: Responding to the needs of diverse learners. *Reading Research Quarterly, 33*, 62-94.

Melaragno, R. J. (1974) Beyond decoding: Systematic schoolwide tutoring in reading. *The Reading Teacher, 27*, 157-60.

O'Donnell, A. M. and Topping, K. J. (1998) Peers assessing peers: Possibilities and problems. In K. J. Topping and S. Ehly (Eds.) *Peer-assisted learning*. Mahwah NJ and London UK: Lawrence Erlbaum Associates.

Phillips, N. B., Hamlett, C. L., Fuchs, L. S. and Fuchs, D. (1993). Combining classwide curriculum-based measurement and peer tutoring to help general educators provide adaptive education. *Learning Disabilities Research and Practice, 8,* 148-156.

Reigert, J. F. (1916). *The Lancasterian system of instruction in the schools of New York city.* New York: Arno Press. (Republished 1969.)

Rohrbeck, C., Ginsburg-Block, M., Fantuzzo, J. and Miller, T. (1999, August 22). *Peer-assisted learning interventions: A meta-analysis.* Paper presented at the annual conference of the American Psychological Association, Washington DC.

Rosenbaum, P. S. (1973). *Peer-mediated instruction.* NY: Teachers' College Press.

Rumelhart, D. E. and Norman, D. A. (1976). *Accretion, tuning and restructuring: Three modes of learning.* La Jolla, CA: Center for Human Information Processing, University of California.

Rumelhart, D. E. and Norman, D. A. (1983). *Representation in memory.* San Diego, CA: Center for Human Information Processing, University of California.

Schunk, D. (1998) Peer modeling. In K. J. Topping and S. Ehly (Eds.) *Peer-assisted learning.* Mahwah NJ and London UK: Lawrence Erlbaum Associates.

Scoble, J., Topping, K. J. and Wigglesworth, C. (1988). Training family and friends as adult literacy tutors. *Journal of Reading, 31 (5),* 410-17. [also in: Radencich, M. C. (Ed.) (1994). Adult literacy. Newark DE: International Reading Association].

Scruggs, T. E., Mastropieri, M. A. and Richter, L. (1985). Peer tutoring with behaviorally disordered students: Social and academic benefits. *Behavioral Disorders, 10 (4),* 283-94.

Scruggs, T. E. and Osguthorpe, R. T. (1986) Tutoring interventions within special education settings: a comparison of cross-age and peer tutoring. *Psychology in the Schools, 23 (2),* 187-93.

Scruggs, T. E. and Mastropieri, M. A. (1998). Tutoring and students with special needs. In K. J. Topping and S. Ehly (Eds.) *Peer-assisted learning.* Mahwah NJ and London UK: Lawrence Erlbaum Associates.

Sharpley, A. M. and Sharpley, C. F. (1981). Peer tutoring: A review of the literature. *Collected Original Resources in Education (CORE) 5 (3),* 7-CI I (fiche 7 and 8). (CORE is produced by Carfax Publishing Company, 35 South Street, Hopkinton, MA 01748 or PO Box 125, Abingdon, Oxfordshire, 0X14 SUE).

Simmons, D., Fuchs, L. and Fuchs, D. (l995). Effects of explicit teaching and peer-mediated instruction on the reading achievement of learning disabled and low-performing students. *Elementary School Journal, 95,* 387-407.

Sindelar, P. T. (1982). The effects of cross-aged tutoring on the comprehension skills of remedial reading students. *The Journal of Special Education, 16 (2),* 199-206.

Skinner, C. H., Shapiro, E. S., Turco, T. L. and Brown, D. K. (1992). A comparison of self-and peer-delivered immediate corrective feedback on multiplication performance. *Journal of School Psychology, 30,* 101-116.

Stowitschek, C., Hecimovic, A., Stowitschek, J. and Shores, R. (1982). Behaviorally disordered adolescents as peer tutors: immediate and generative effects on instructional performance and spelling achievement. *Behavioral Disorders, 7,* 136-48.

Strain, P. S. (Ed.) (1981). *The utilization of classroom peers as behavior change agents.* New York: Plenum Press.

Topping, K. J. (1987). Peer tutored paired reading: outcome data from ten projects. *Educational Psychology, 7 (2),* 133-45. [Also in: S. Goodlad & B. Hirst (Eds.) (1990) Explorations in Peer Tutoring. Oxford: Blackwell).

Topping, K. J. (1988). *The peer tutoring handbook: Promoting co-operative learning.* London: Croom Helm; Cambridge MA: Brookline Books. [Also in translation as: Insegnamento Reciproco Tra Compagni. (1997). Trento: Erickson).

Topping, K. J. (1995). *Paired reading, spelling & writing: The handbook for teachers and parents*. London and New York: Cassell.

Topping, K. J. (1997). *Duolog reading: Video training pack*. Madison, WI: Institute for Academic Excellence.

Topping, K. J. (1998a). Paired learning in literacy. In K. J. Topping and S. Ehly (Eds.) *Peer-assisted learning*. Mahwah NJ and London UK: Lawrence Erlbaum Associates.

Topping, K. J. (1998b). *The paired science handbook: parental involvement and peer tutoring in science*. London: Fulton; Bristol PA: Taylor & Francis.

Topping, K. J. (1998c). Peer assessment between students in college and university. *Review of Educational Research, 68 (3)*, 249-276.

Topping, K. J. (2001). *Thinking, reading, writing: a practical guide to paired learning with peers, parents & volunteers*. New York & London: Continuum International.

Topping, K. J. & Bamford, J. (1998). *Parental involvement and peer tutoring in mathematics and science: developing paired maths into paired science*. London: Fulton; Bristol PA: Taylor & Francis.

Topping, K. J. & Bamford, J. (1998). *The paired maths handbook: parental involvement and peer tutoring in mathematics*. London: Fulton; Bristol PA: Taylor & Francis.

Topping, K. J. and Ehly, S. (Eds.) (1998). *Peer-assisted learning*. Mahwah NJ and London UK: Lawrence Erlbaum Associates.

Topping, K. J. and Wolfendale, S. W. (Eds.) (1985). *Parental involvement in children's reading*. New York: Nichols; London: Croom Helm.

Towler, L. and Broadfoot, P. (1992). Self-assessment in the primary school. *Educational Review, 44 (2)*, 137-151.

Wheldall, K. and Mettem, P. (1985). Behavioural peer tutoring: Training 16-year-old tutors to employ the "Pause, Prompt and Praise" method with 12-year-old remedial readers. *Educational Psychology, 5 (1)*, 27-44.

Wilkes, R. (1975). *Peer and cross-age tutoring and related topics: an annotated bibliography.* (ERIC Document ED 115372)

Wolfendale, S. W. and Topping, K. J. (Eds.) (1996). *Family involvement in literacy: Effective partnerships in education.* London and New York: Cassell.

Zimmerman, B. J. (1990). Self-regulated learning and academic achievement: An overview. *Educational Psychologist, 25*, 3-17.

WITHDRAWN